S0-BDL-556

J.R.R. Tolkien

J.R.R. Tolkien

These and other titles are included in The Importance Of biography series:

Maya Angelou	Ernest Hemingway
Louis Armstrong	Adolf Hitler
Neil Armstrong	Thomas Jefferson
James Baldwin	John F. Kennedy
Lucille Ball	Martin Luther King Jr.
The Beatles	Bruce Lee
Alexander Graham Bell	Lenin
Napoleon Bonaparte	John Lennon
Julius Caesar	Abraham Lincoln
Rachel Carson	Charles Lindbergh
Fidel Castro	Douglas MacArthur
Charlie Chaplin	Margaret Mead
Charlemagne	Golda Meir
Winston Churchill	Mother Teresa
Hillary Rodham Clinton	Muhammad
Christopher Columbus	John Muir
Leonardo da Vinci	Richard M. Nixon
James Dean	Pablo Picasso
Charles Dickens	Edgar Allan Poe
Walt Disney	Queen Elizabeth I
Dr. Seuss	Franklin D. Roosevelt
F. Scott Fitzgerald	Jonas Salk
Henry Ford	Margaret Sanger
Anne Frank	William Shakespeare
Benjamin Franklin	Frank Sinatra
Mohandas Gandhi	Tecumseh
John Glenn	J.R.R. Tolkien
Jane Goodall	Simon Wiesenthal
Martha Graham	The Wright Brothers
Lorraine Hansberry	Chuck Yeager

THE IMPORTANCE OF

J.R.R. Tolkien

by Stuart P. Levine

LUCENT
BOOKS®

THOMSON
™
GALE

San Diego • Detroit • New York • San Francisco • Cleveland • New Haven, Conn. • Waterville, Maine • London • Munich

LIBRARY OF CONGRESS CATALOGING-IN-PUBLICATION DATz

Levine, Stuart P., 1968
  J.R.R. Tolkien / by Stuart P. Levine.
    p. cm. — (The importance of)
Summary: Describes the life and work of the renowned British fantasy writer, creator of
the world of hobbits and Middle Earth, and author of "The Lord of the Rings" trilogy.
Includes bibliographical references and index.
  ISBN 1-59018-356-8 (hardback : alk. paper)
  1. Tolkien, J.R.R. (John Ronald Reuel), 1892-1973—Juvenile literature. 2. Fantasy fic-
tion, English—History and criticism—Juvenile literature. 3. Authors, English—20thcen-
tury—Biography—Juvenile literature. 4. Philologists—Great Britian—biography—Juvenile literature. 5. Middle Earth (Imaginary place)—Juvenile literature. [1. Tolkein, J.R.R.
(John Ronale Reuel), 1892-1973. 2. Authors, English]
  I. Title. II. Series.
  PR6039.032Z58 2004
  828'.91209—dc22
                                                                          2003013850

Printed in the United States of America

Contents

Foreword

THE IMPORTANCE OF biography series deals with individuals who have made a unique contribution to history. The editors of the series have deliberately chosen to cast a wide net and include people from all fields of endeavor. Individuals from politics, music, art, literature, philosophy, science, sports, and religion are all represented. In addition, the editors did not restrict the series to individuals whose accomplishments have helped change the course of history. Of necessity, this criterion would have eliminated many whose contribution was great, though limited. Charles Darwin, for example, was responsible for radically altering the scientific view of the natural history of the world. His achievements continue to impact the study of science today. Others, such as Chief Joseph of the Nez Percé, played a pivotal role in the history of their own people. While Joseph's influence does not extend much beyond the Nez Percé, his nonviolent resistance to white expansion and his continuing role in protecting his tribe and his homeland remain an inspiration to all.

These biographies are more than factual chronicles. Each volume attempts to emphasize an individual's contributions both in his or her own time and for posterity. For example, the voyages of Christopher Columbus opened the way to European colonization of the New World. Unquestionably, his encounter with the New World brought monumental changes to both Europe and the Americas in his day. Today, however, the broader impact of Columbus's voyages is being critically scrutinized. *Christopher Columbus*, as well as every biography in The Importance Of series, includes and evaluates the most recent scholarship available on each subject.

Each author includes a wide variety of primary and secondary source quotations to document and substantiate his or her work. All quotes are footnoted to show readers exactly how and where biographers derive their information, as well as provide stepping stones to further research. These quotations enliven the text by giving readers eyewitness views of the life and times of each individual covered in The Importance Of series.

Finally, each volume is enhanced by photographs, bibliographies, chronologies, and comprehensive indexes. For both the casual reader and the student engaged in research, The Importance Of biographies will be a fascinating adventure into the lives of people who have helped shape humanity's past and present, and who will continue to shape its future.

IMPORTANT DATES IN THE LIFE OF J.R.R. TOLKIEN

1892
John Ronald Reuel Tolkien is born January 3 in Bloemfontein, South Africa.

1904
Mother dies and the boys move in with their aunt, though they are given into the legal custody of Father Frances Xavier Morgan.

1936
Delivers famous lecture, "*Beowulf*: The Monsters and the Critics."

1895
Ronald, along with his mother and brother, returns to Birmingham, England.

1915
Graduates from college and enlists in the British army.

1931
The Inklings come together for the first time.

1929
Daughter, Priscilla, is born.

1890	1900	1910	1920	1930

1896
Father dies in South Africa; the Tolkien family moves to the quiet English countryside of Sarehole.

1911
Formation of the T.C.B.S.; in the autumn, Tolkien begins his term at Exeter College.

1926
Meets and befriend C.S. Lewis and fou a new club known the Coalbiters.

1916
Marries Edith Mary Bratt and immediately ships out overseas to begin a tour of duty on the front lines of World War I; becomes sick with trench fever and returns to England.

1925
Returns to Oxford to a a position as professor Anglo-Saxon studies.

1917
Begins work on the history and mythology of Middle Earth (later released as *The Silmarillion*); first son, John, is born.

1924
Raised to professor of Eng language at Leeds; third s Christopher, is born.

1918
Begins work at the offices of the *Oxford English Dictionary*.

1920
Appointed reader in English language at Leeds University; second son, Michael, is born.

1937
The Hobbit is released and Tolkien begins work on the sequel that will eventually become *The Lord of the Rings.*

1939
Delivers his lecture "On Fairy Stories" at St. Andrew's University.

1954
Volumes 1 and 2 of *The Lord of the Rings* are published.

1955
Volume 3 of *The Lord of the Rings* is published.

1959
Retires from teaching.

1977
Christopher Tolkien completes his father's work and publishes *The Silmarillion.*

1940   **1950**   **1960**   **1970**   **1980**

1945
Becomes professor of English language and literature at Oxford.

1965
Ace releases an unauthorized paperback edition of *The Lord of the Rings* and the popularity of the work surges.

1973
Dies September 2 at the age of eighty-one.

1968
The Tolkiens move to Bournemouth to escape fans and journalists.

1972
Tolkien returns to Oxford, where he lives out his final years on the campus of Merton College; awarded the CBE by the queen of England, and an honorary doctorate of letters by Oxford University.

1971
Edith Mary Tolkien dies at the age of eighty-two.

The Man Behind the Rings

J.R.R. Tolkien is often described as the father of the modern fantasy novel. His epic *The Lord of the Rings* has even been ranked as the greatest book of the twentieth century. Critical opinion of Tolkien's achievement is sharply divided, however. When a 1996 poll of twenty-six thousand readers, organized by Waterstone's Booksellers and the BBC, reported the number one ranking, critics demanded a recount. Nevertheless, four subsequent polls conducted by four independent groups—ranging from newspapers to the Nestle Chocolate company—produced the same result when respondents were asked to list their favorite novels of the twentieth century.

Though literary critics seem to either love or hate Tolkien's masterwork, the message of his fans has been loud and clear for nearly fifty years. Having sold more than 100 million copies, *The Lord of the Rings* is certainly one of the most well known works of fiction in recent history and Tolkien one of the most famous writers. However, the man who conjured up this epic tale of heroic fantasy lived a very quiet and surprisingly simple life. Most of his own grand adventures occurred within the confines of his incredible imagination.

THE LORD OF LANGUAGES

Tolkien is primarily remembered for writing *The Lord of the Rings*, a book he did not publish until the age of sixty-two. He spent nearly his entire adult life creating the history and mythology of the world in which the story would take place, Middle Earth, a land filled with elves, dragons, and magic, but possessing nonetheless remarkable similarities to our own world. What many people do not know about Tolkien is that he also spent these years gaining recognition as one of the world's leading professors of philology, the study of languages and their development. This expertise would define his fiction, which developed from the many languages Tolkien invented.

From an early age, Tolkien was fascinated with the origins of language and the cultures that created them. By the age of sixteen he had become a prodigy, with an understanding of the basics of eight languages, and even a few attempts at inventing new ones. As an undergraduate at Oxford University, he continued to study philology and began more serious work toward the creation of a fully developed language of his own. Based on what he considered to be the most beautiful language in the world, Finnish, it eventually developed into the tongue spoken by the elves that would populate his fictional world.

After brief service in World War I and a period on the faculty of Leeds University, Tolkien returned to Oxford and carved out a niche for himself as one of the world's foremost authorities on Middle English, an extinct language spoken from the twelfth through sixteenth centuries. During his time at Oxford, he befriended another professor, the well-known fantasy author C.S. Lewis—author of *The Lion, the Witch, and the Wardrobe*—and together they formed a club known as the Inklings. Throughout Tolkien's life he belonged to a number of men's literary clubs, but the Inklings was by far the most important. Lasting more than thirty years, it would be the sounding board for all his work and the society in which both he and Lewis refined the stories they spent their lives creating.

THE MYTHMAKER

When Tolkien was twenty-five years old, he began creating what he hoped would be a mythology for England. Condensed

J.R.R. Tolkien was a student, professor, and soldier before publishing his most famous work, The Lord of the Rings.

and later released as *The Silmarillion*, he considered this his life's work, though it was not published until after his death. At age forty-five, however, Tolkien saw his first commercial success with *The Hobbit*. The story was based on engaging creatures who resembled very small, simple humans. As millions came to know, hobbits stand no more than half the height of a person and do not like to stray too far from home. Because hobbits have a deep love of simple foods, good

Fantasy author C.S. Lewis and Tolkien often shared their work with each other.

ale, and a pipe to smoke, many people—including Tolkien—have commented that they were modeled on the author himself. Even the land they lived in, known as the Shire, was very much like the quiet English countryside where Tolkien grew up. He referred to the Shire as a place where "there was less noise and more green."[1]

As he got older, he became an increasingly outspoken critic of modern industrialization and the methodical destruction of the natural world. He was a staunch environmentalist before such attitudes were fashionable. His hobbits, who loved the trees and gardens of the world as much as he did, became quite popular, and when both his fans and publishers demanded a sequel, he set to work.

THE UNEXPECTED ICON

For the next two decades he became completely absorbed in "discovering" a story he claims was not invented, but revealed to him as a true history by divine influence. When the resulting book, *The Lord of the Rings*, was finally published seventeen years later, he was pleased with its initial success and certainly with the financial freedom it gave him for the first time in his life. He lovingly answered the stacks of letters he received from his ardent fans.

Tolkien's The Lord of Rings *trilogy has been translated into many languages and has influenced the works of many fantasy authors.*

However, the attention soon became overwhelming. As his popularity soared, Tolkien found his quiet English home invaded by a never-ending parade of fans and journalists. He became a reluctant icon of the 1960s youth counterculture and was confused—sometimes angered and sometimes amused—by the messages people read into his work. After his retirement from Oxford, he and his wife moved to a remote area on the coast of England, where he could escape the limelight in relative peace.

PAVING THE WAY

Perhaps the greatest legacy of J.R.R. Tolkien was his influence on both the form and the commercial success of fantasy literature.

The incredible attention to detail Tolkien put into the creation of his Middle Earth—inventing complete languages, family histories, detailed geographies, and entire races of creatures complete with finely tuned descriptions of their physical appearance, strengths and weaknesses, and even concepts of spirituality—became the standard by which all other fantasy authors were judged. The influence of his work can be clearly seen in the works of countless fantasy authors such as Robert Jordan's *Wheel of Time* books, Terry Brooks's *Shannara* chronicles, and J.K. Rowlings's *Harry Potter* series. In addition to its influence on the content and style of modern fantasy, the success of *The Lord of the Rings* created an entirely new niche—adult fantasy—in the literary market. It demonstrated the potential for the genre's commercial success and paved the way for the hundreds of fantasy novels that line the shelves of bookstores today.

Though Tolkien always warned people not to read messages—or, even worse, allegory—into his stories, he certainly infused his writing with the strong views he had developed in life. He once said "One writes such a story not out of the leaves of trees still to be observed, . . . but it grows like a seed in the dark out of the leaf-mould of the mind: Out of all that has been seen or thought or read, that has long ago been forgotten, descending into the deeps."[2]

The events of J.R.R. Tolkien's long life clearly influenced his epic fiction. Examining the role these events played gives a unique insight into the mind and the life of a man many consider to be one of the world's greatest storytellers.

1 A Country Boy

J.R.R. Tolkien was an Englishman to the core. He took enormous pride in the history, traditions, and very landscape of the British Isles. He rarely felt the desire or found the occasion to travel abroad. However, this embodiment of the English gentleman was actually born and raised, for the first few years of his life, many thousands of miles from his ancestral home, in South Africa.

THE FAR END OF THE _____

Arthur Reuel Tolkien, _____ s father, worked at Lloyd's Bank i____ n while engaged to Tolkien's mo____ bel Suffield. They were in love but fo___ den to marry until they were older and Arthur was financially stable, a situation in which their son would find himself nearly twenty years later. As business was slow at Lloyd's, Arthur decided to seek out new opportunities to make his fortune at the outer reaches of the British Empire. He took a position at the Bank of Africa, in British-controlled South Africa. Life was not easy so far away from his home and loved ones, but Arthur was determined. After a year of hard work, he was promoted to manager of the bank's primary branch in Bloemfontein. At about this same time, Mabel turned twenty-one and set sail to join her fiancé. Soon after she arrived, on April 16, 1891, Arthur and Mabel were married. On January 3, 1892 of the following year, they welcomed their first child, John Ronald Reuel Tolkien. Ronald, as he was called, was born slightly premature but was otherwise healthy. Writing to her mother-in-law back home, Mabel described him as looking like "a fairy when he's very much dressed-up in white frills and white shoes. When he's very much undressed I think he looks more of an elf still."[3]

Two years later, Ronald's brother, Hilary Reuel, was born. Though Arthur enjoyed the African wilderness, Mabel missed her home and her family. By the age of three Ronald had become ill and Mabel was increasingly unhappy in South Africa. When the doctor informed her that the hot, dry climate was not helping Ronald's health, she decided it was time for them to move home to England.

In April 1895 Mabel and the two boys returned to England and moved in temporarily with relatives in Birmingham. Arthur stayed behind to attend to business matters, planning to join his family in a few months. Before he could return, however, he became

THE FAR END OF THE EMPIRE

J.R.R. Tolkien spent the first three years of his life in South Africa, at the far reaches of the British Empire. Tolkien recalled on numerous occasions that life there was difficult but full of adventure.

The Tolkiens lived in the dry grasslands of central South Africa, home to lions, jackals, wild dogs, and hyenas. Life on this frontier was an exciting challenge to Ronald's father. His mother, however, found life there less to her liking and missed the familiar comforts of England. Ronald seemed to thrive there despite a number of misadventures. As a baby, he was apparently "abducted" by one of the African house servants. The servant, a black man named Isaak, had actually just "borrowed" the baby to take to his village and show off the white infant as a novelty. By the time Isaak returned with Ronald later that day, the family was in a panic, but so relieved to find him safe that Isaak was not fired. The grateful Isaak later named his own child Isaak Mr. Tolkien Victor (Victor being a reference to Queen Victoria).

At the age of two, while playing outside near the house, Ronald was bitten by a tarantula. His nurse reportedly sucked the venom out and no harm was done, but much later in life, giant, menacing spiders—such as the terrifying Shelob, which poisons Frodo in *Lord of the Rings*—would play a prominent role in his fiction.

ill and the months became nearly a year. In February 1896, he was still recovering and unable to travel, so Mabel decided she would return to Africa with the children to look after him. Just a few days later, however, Arthur Tolkien died without ever seeing England or his children again.

LIFE IN THE SHIRE

Arthur had left little inheritance, so Mabel remained with her parents for a short time while figuring out what her next step would be. During this time, Ronald became very close to his mother's family. His paternal grandfather lived just down the road, but he died just six months after Arthur and his grandchildren never knew him well. As Tolkien said later in life, "Though a Tolkien by name, I am Suffield by tastes, talents, and upbringing."[4]

By the summer of 1896, when Ronald was four years old, his mother had found a place she could afford to rent with her meager savings and some financial help from her family. It was in a hamlet just outside of Birmingham, known as Sarehole. The next four years in this little village would have a profound effect on the young Tolkien.

Sarehole was a place right out of a storybook, nestled in pristine English countryside, complete with farms, rolling hills, open fields with wildflowers, ponds with white swans, large oak trees, a stream, and even an old mill that ground corn. Ronald and his brother were in heaven. They spent their days roaming the countryside, having grand adventures. These experiences planted the seed of what would eventually become the Shire, the country of his fictional hobbits. Described in his books as an unspoiled pastoral land of green fields and simple beauty, as Tolkien puts it, "The Shire is based on rural England and no other country in the world."[5]

THE YOUNG SCHOLAR

Mabel Tolkien refused to let her financial limitations hinder her boys' opportunity to get a good education and make something of their lives. In fact, she set her sights quite high. Despite her academically isolated country life and her lack of funds, she was determined to see her boys attend King Edward's School, the finest private school in West Midlands County. The entrance exams were difficult, however, and the boys needed very high scores to have any chance of earning a scholarship, which would most likely be the only way they could afford to attend.

Having been a governess before she married, Mabel took on the task of tutoring the boys at home in their early years, in preparation for their entrance exams. She found this an easy task with Ronald, as he was a very willing student. He absorbed everything she taught him. By the age of four, he was reading on his own; once he had mastered English, she began to teach him the basics of Latin and French. Even then he showed a precocious fascination for the sounds of words. Mabel also introduced him to art, for which he seemed to have some talent. Drawing landscapes was his favorite subject, and later in life, he became quite good, supplying his own illustrations in several of his books, including *The Hobbit*.

THE BEAUTY OF TREES

Next Mabel Tolkien turned to botany. This was a subject Ronald took to nearly as well as language. As with words, he showed an aptitude for learning about the science and classifications of plants, but what really interested him was the way a plant looked and felt. He especially loved trees. To the end of his life he would spend hours sitting by them, feeling them, and even talking to them. A friend of Tolkien's, Lord Halsbury, recalled a time when they had been on a walk together and Tolkien began instructing the man on how to communicate with a tree: "[Tolkien] stood up to the tree, put his forehead against the bark, put both hands on either side of the bowl of the tree, and was absolutely silent with his eyes shut, for a little while."[6] Afterward, he turned to his friend to share the "message" the tree had given him.

Lord Halsbury refused to reveal to anyone just what that message was.

Mabel instilled a deep respect for trees and plants in her son. His attachment to wildlife became a near obsession, surely rooted in his days in Sarehole. He recalled one occasion from his youth that seemed to leave a lasting impression on him: "There was a willow hanging over the mill-pool and I learned to climb it. It belonged to a butcher on the Stratford Road, I think. One day they cut it down. They didn't do anything with it: the log just lay there. I never forgot that."[7] This sadness and confusion associated with the felling of trees would remain with him throughout his life and feature prominently in his books. In *The Lord of the Rings,* he even created a species of trees, known as Ents, with the strength, mobility, and sentience to revolt against the nature-hating wizard, Saruman.

Nineteenth-century author George MacDonald was young J.R.R. Tolkien's favorite writer.

THE WORLD OF FANTASY

Another aspect of young Tolkien's education revolved around books. His mother encouraged him to read often. He enjoyed reading, especially stories that involved creatures and worlds of fantasy. As a child, Tolkien's favorite author was George MacDonald, a nineteenth-century writer often cited as one of the earliest precursors of modern fantasy whose works concerned goblins, fairies, and other mythical creatures. MacDonald (along with William Morris, whom Tolkien would discover later in life) was a strong influence on Tolkien. Among other favorites were Andrew Lang's Fairy Books. The one he read most often was the Red Fairy Book, which contained a story about a dragon named

Fafnir and the knight Sigurd who pursued him. Arthurian legends were another favorite; Tolkien would soon find that anything connected with the mythology of England fascinated him. As Ronald's love for these stories grew, he began to invent some of his own. By the age of seven, he was writing his own dragon stories. During this time, a classic mythological image appeared to him, not in a book, but in his dreams. He had recurring nightmares about a great ocean sweeping over a green field, enveloping and drowning all the trees and the land. He would later refer to this as his Atlantis complex, as he was always fascinated by the Atlantean myths of an ancient advanced civilization rumored to have been swallowed by the sea. Later, this concept would appear in his fiction as the doomed island nation of Númenor.

Andrew Lang wrote a series of books called the Fairy Books that Tolkien enjoyed as a child.

KING EDWARD'S

Eventually Ronald passed the entrance exams to King Edward's. His mother was thrilled, but he did not win a scholarship. They would not have been able to afford the tuition if not for a kindhearted uncle on Arthur's side of the family who had a soft spot for Arthur's children and paid much of the boy's way to school.

Unfortunately, the school was four miles from their home in Sarehole and they could not afford the daily train fare. As her sons' education was a primary concern, Mabel packed the boys up and moved to a suburb of Birmingham, known as Moseley, nearer the school. Ronald was distraught at leaving his country paradise, but he would get one more brief chance to return to that life in just a few years.

Tolkien proved an apt pupil and enjoyed the amenities offered by King Edward's

School. However, he described his house in Moseley as dreadful. Ronald had a difficult time adjusting to life so near the industrial city of Birmingham, with its soot-darkened streets and plumes of black smoke rising from its numerous factories.

However, amid the noise and smoke, he discovered a kind of beauty he had never known before. Sitting at his bedroom window, he would watch coal trucks pass by on their way to and from the district of Wales. The names on the side of the trucks were in Welsh, a language he had never seen or heard. He found names of towns like Nantyglo, Senghenydd, and Tredegar fascinating and even beautiful, rolling the sounds over his tongue again and again. Ronald always had a distinct interest in languages, but this was the first time he felt truly mesmerized by the sounds of words.

FATHER FRANCIS

In the years since Arthur's death, Mabel had become increasingly involved in religion. The Anglican Church of England, a major Protestant denomination, was by far the dominant religion of Britain, and both the Tolkiens and the Suffields were members. However, Mabel's sister May Incledon began to develop an interest in the Roman Catholic faith and brought Mabel with her to church. Mabel eventually developed a belief in Catholicism that she never felt as a Protestant. Eventually, Mabel's faith grew very powerful and she announced to her family that she was converting. The family was outraged and cut her off from their lives. This loss was a blow to Mabel

and the withdrawal of the family's financial support meant a new level of hardship for her and the boys.

Having trouble making ends meet, and wanting the boys to have a proper Catholic education, Mabel removed them from King Edward's and moved them to a small house near the Birmingham Oratory, where Mabel had been attending church. Attached to the small church was the Oratory School of St. Philip. At the Birmingham Oratory, they met and befriended a priest, Francis Xavier Morgan.

Father Francis, as he was known, was an extraordinarily kind man with a booming voice and a wonderful sense of humor. Young children, including the Tolkiens, were often frightened by his loud, boisterous manner when they first met him, but they usually became extremely fond of him. As the priest was half-Welsh and half-Spanish, Ronald was drawn to him right away. Father Francis took an immediate liking to the entire Tolkien family and became a father figure to the boys.

Mabel and her sons were very happy with their life at the Oratory, immersing themselves in the daily activities of the church. However, it quickly became apparent that St. Philip's was not able to provide Ronald with the academic stimulation he needed. After just one year at the school, and with financial assistance from Father Francis, he was back at King Edward's.

FAITH AND LOSS

In the midst of their more settled, happy lives, Mabel's health began to decline. For

A Childhood Paradise Spoiled

In J.R.R. Tolkien: A Biography, Humphrey Carpenter describes Tolkien's return to his beloved country home of Sarehole, at the age of forty-one. Tolkien recorded in his diary the horror he felt at seeing the way it had changed.

"[We traveled] down what is left of beloved lanes of childhood, and past the very gate of our cottage, now in the midst of a sea of new red-brick. The old mill still stands, and Mrs. Hunt's still sticks out into the road as it turns uphill; but the crossing beyond the now fenced-in pool, where the bluebell lane ran down into the mill lane, is now a dangerous crossing alive with motors and red lights. The White Ogre's house (which the children were excited to see) is become a petrol station, and most of Short Avenue and the elms between it and the crossing have gone. How I envy those whose precious early scenery has not been exposed to such violent and peculiarly hideous change."

Tolkien grew up in this house in Sarehole, near Birmingham, England.

Edith Bratt and Tolkien met at a boardinghouse for orphans. The two developed a friendship and later fell in love.

ther Francis arranged for the whole family to stay for the summer at a little cottage owned by the church. This cottage was in Rednal, a country town very much like their home in Sarehole. The family was back in the Shire as far as young Ronald was concerned. With his mother's health improving and frequent visits from Father Francis, the summer of 1904 was a beautiful time for him.

Unfortunately, his return to paradise was brief. Within a few months, his mother's health began to decline again and by November of that year, she slipped into a diabetic coma and died. At the age of twelve, he had lost the only family he had ever known and been forced again to leave the English countryside and return to Birmingham.

This event had a profound effect on young Ronald's life, cementing his faith in the Catholic religion. Mabel had left Father Francis as the boys' legal guardian, so his role as a father figure grew. Under his guidance, Ronald developed an even stronger connection to the church. In addition, he believed that his mother had died for her commitment to the church. Tolkien felt that the financial and social hardships placed upon Mabel, when her family ostracized her for converting to Catholicism, were strong factors contributing to her declining health and even-

some time, she had suffered the effects of diabetes, a disease that today can be managed with medication, but at that time was life threatening. In April 1904, Mabel entered the hospital and the boys had to live with relatives for several months.

By the summer, she was well enough to leave the hospital but still needed rest. Fatual death. Rather then reject Catholicism for this, he felt that he had an obligation to carry on her faith, as it was so important to her. He saw her as a martyr and, in a letter to a friend many years later, he wrote that he "witnessed the heroic sufferings and early death . . . of my mother who brought me into the Church; and received the astonishing charity of Francis Morgan. . . . I fell in love with the Blessed Sacrament from the beginning—and by the mercy of God never have fallen out again."[8]

With his mother's death, a gloomier side of Ronald emerged. Until then, Ronald had been a cheerful boy. His mother was his entire world. Losing her and leaving the unspoiled English country life again may very well have felt like being expelled from Eden. He would be a different person from that day forward. From the age of twelve and through the rest of his life, friends would describe him as having an almost split personality. At most times, he remained a jovial, social, and generally happy person. But he developed a dark and brooding side as well. From his journal entries throughout the rest of his life, one might be led to believe that this darker side had taken over his entire personality. His entries were almost always of a pessimistic nature, dwelling on things he hated or feared in life. However, a closer analysis reveals that he seems to have used his journal as a repository for these feelings, only making entries when he was in these foul moods. In his more jovial moods, he was out and about with people socializing rather than writing down his feelings. He would spend the rest of his life alternating between joy and sorrow.

Though Tolkien never again lived in his revered English countryside, his imagination would allow him to return time and again as he re-created a similar world in his fiction for his hobbits.

LIFE MARCHES ON

Father Francis arranged for the brothers to live with their Aunt Beatrice. At school, Ronald befriended a young man named Christopher Wiseman with whom he had much in common, including a shared interest in mythology, languages, and rugby. Both boys were academically minded and enjoyed a good-natured competitive spirit. They would remain close friends for the rest of their lives.

He was beginning to return to some semblance of normalcy in his life, making friends, playing sports, and indulging in his studies. However, neither he nor his brother were entirely fond of Aunt Beatrice. She was not the warm and caring person their mother had been and she was ill-equipped to care for two rambunctious teenage boys. Father Francis decided the boys might be happier somewhere else. At the age of sixteen, Tolkien moved into a boardinghouse for orphans like himself. The house, run by a Mrs. Faulkner, was affiliated with the Birmingham Oratory and had Father Francis's approval.

One of the other orphans was a girl named Edith Bratt. At nineteen, Edith was three years older than Ronald but the pair had an instant rapport. They enjoyed spending time together and found that they had a lot in common, not least of which was family loss. Within a short time, they became good friends and allies against Mrs. Faulkner, who, as it turned out, could be very difficult at times.

Typically, meals at the boardinghouse were not lavish and the boys were always hungry. Edith conspired with one of the cooks to steal extra food and sneak it up to the Tolkien boys. Their mischief also extended to sitting on the second floor balcony and tossing sugar cubes into the large hats of the people walking below.

Friendship soon turned to infatuation and they decided they were in love. One day, however, while on a bike ride together in the country, their secret romance was discovered and reported to Father Francis, who objected to the relationship as highly improper. The couple lived under the same roof, she was almost twenty, and he was supposed to be focused on his work and studying for the Oxford University entrance exams. Father Francis moved the boys out of the house and insisted that Ronald and Edith end their romance immediately.

Ronald's only joy in recent times had been with Edith. Against his conscience and better judgment, he began seeing her in secret. When he failed his first set of college entrance exams that year, Father Francis learned of the ongoing relationship and was outraged. He had made a significant financial and emotional investment in Ronald's future and he felt that the youth was wasting it in this infatuation. Father Francis forbade Ronald to see or even communicate with Edith again until he was twenty-one and no longer under his guardianship. Ronald complied, but when Edith decided to move from Birmingham, Ronald wrote in his diary that that he was extremely depressed.

Though Tolkien would always feel a debt of gratitude toward Father Francis for the way he took him in and guided him, this episode put a lasting wedge in their relationship. He would later recall that the decree placed upon him regarding Edith turned a childhood infatuation into an enduring love. He was not about to give up on Edith. At this point, however, he had no choice but to take Father Francis's advice to devote himself to his studies and his next set of entrance exams to Oxford.

2 Unlocking the Doors of Language

With Edith's departure, Ronald began to focus on his studies. He had varied interests at school but was always partial to anything that involved words and language. He and his cousins had already been playfully inventing languages of their own. The first, called Animalic, was composed primarily of a vocabulary of animal names. The second, Nevbosh, was a slightly more sophisticated attempt at real language creation. He and his cousins even wrote limericks in Nevbosh:

> Dar fys ma vel gom co palt "
> Hoc Pys go iskili far maino woc?
> Pro si go fys do roc de
> Do cat ym maino bocte
> De volt fact soc ma taimful gyroc!"

> There was an old man who said,
> "How Can I possibly carry my cow?
> For if I were to ask it
> To get in my basket
> It would make such a terrible row!"[9]

His passion for languages seemed to have no limits. In high school, one of Ronald's English teachers, George Brewerton, introduced him to both his past and his future, in the form of Middle English.

The English language has changed and evolved over nearly two thousand years into the form spoken in today's world. Middle English, spoken from about A.D. 1100 through 1500, is a very different language from Modern English. One day in his English language and literature class, Brewerton read Chaucer's medieval *Canterbury Tales* aloud in the original Middle English. Ronald was enraptured by the collected stories of peasants and nobles traveling across fourteenth-century England. He was fascinated by the notion that this language, and adventures such as these, were those of his own ancestors.

LANGUAGES OF OLD AND NEW

Ronald was so taken with Middle English that he asked Brewerton for a primer, or basic rule book, to help him study it. His fascination with the fact that his ancestors had spoken this tongue so many centuries ago, right here in his home of West Midland County, would become a cornerstone of his life. According to Tolkien, "I am a West-midlander by blood, and took to early West-midland Middle English as to a known tongue as soon as I set eyes on it."[10] He quickly absorbed the roots of

Geoffrey Chaucer's Canterbury Tales *inspired Tolkien to take up the study of Middle English.*

Middle English and began to enjoy it even more as he discovered original texts such as *Sir Gawain and the Green Knight.* He then began to look for even older texts and learned some simple phrases in Old English (spoken from A.D. 450 through 1100).

Through Brewerton's primers, he even began to learn a little Old Norse, also known as Icelandic. In Icelandic, he found a language that appealed not only to his sense of history, but also to his sense of beauty. Much like the few words he had seen on coal trucks in Welsh, Icelandic had a certain lyrical quality that Ronald was innately drawn to. He became absorbed in studying the elemental roots of languages, and piecing together the connective tissue that bound them together. By the time he was sixteen, he understood the basics of at least eight languages.

GOTHIC

As Ronald learned more about real languages, he continued to work on creating his own. After his crude attempts with Animalic and Nevbosh, he moved on to a more sophisticated language, which he called Naffarin. Naffarin had not only vocabulary but syntax and rules of pronunciation.

Ronald's work on Naffarin came to a halt one day in Father Francis's library when he came across *The Primer of Gothic Language* by Joseph Wright. This was an invaluable discovery, as Gothic was a completely dead language and presented a tantalizing linguistic mystery. Unlike other old languages, such as Latin, no one living could completely understand or read Gothic. The primer revealed that only fragments of the language still existed. In fact, no one had a clear understanding of exactly where it had even come from. Ronald immersed himself in the study of Gothic immediately, absorbed by the question of who had spoken this language. What had their lives been like? Why did their way of life and their language die?

Eventually, he began to fill in the missing parts of the language by making up vocabulary that seemed to fit the other structural elements in the primer. However, his obsession went further. In order to invent words that made sense, he found that he had to go backward in linguistic time and create the roots, or hypothetical precursors, for the Gothic language that would (or could) give rise to the newly patched together version of it he was creating.

He spent hours on end in this endeavor. His friend Christopher, who was studying ancient Egyptian hieroglyphics at the time, took an avid interest in this mad hobby. The more Ronald worked on Gothic and its unnamed antecedent, the more he began to wonder about the lives and history of the people who may have spoken it. This same question plagued him wherever he

GRAMMAR OF THE
GOTHIC LANGUAGE

AND

THE GOSPEL OF ST. MARK
SELECTIONS FROM THE OTHER GOSPELS
AND THE SECOND EPISTLE TO TIMOTHY
WITH NOTES AND GLOSSARY

BY

JOSEPH WRIGHT

PH.D., D.C.L., LL.D., LITT.D.

Fellow of the British Academy
Corpus Christi Professor of Comparative Philology
in the University of Oxford

SECOND EDITION WITH A
SUPPLEMENT TO THE GRAMMAR

BY

O. L. SAYCE, M.A.

Lecturer in German in the University of Oxford

OXFORD
AT THE CLARENDON PRESS

After discovering Joseph Wright's Grammar of the Gothic Language, *Tolkien immersed himself in the study of Gothic.*

found gaps in other languages. For example, only a few surviving original texts of Old English were available from which to piece together the history that had created it. His fascination with the mysteries of this kind of linguistic anthropology would remain with him throughout his life and would help shape not only his professional career, but also the fiction he later wrote. The whole of Middle Earth was actually created to help him figure out who had spoken Quenya, one of fourteen fully or partially invented languages.

The Star Pupil

Ronald became something of a prodigy where languages were concerned. His prep school debate society upheld a tradition in which one debate each year would be delivered in Latin, as all students were required to study it. Tolkien took this practice to the extreme. When representing a Greek ambassador in another debate, he presented all his positions and rebuttals in ancient Greek. Later in the semester, he delivered a speech in Anglo-Saxon (another name for Old English) and on one occasion he embraced the role of a barbarian envoy to the Senate by speaking in fluent Gothic.

In an English class, he delivered a lecture he had prepared entitled *The Modern Languages of Europe—Derivations and Capabilities.* After the third hour of the lecture, his teacher had to cut him off. He was only half-finished. Another English teacher at King Edward's, R.W. Reynolds, introduced him to the concept of literary criticism. He found that his natural attraction to languages was made even richer when he moved beyond simply learning a language and began studying the literature that had been written in it.

He began to read his old childhood stories about Fafnir the dragon and Sigurd the knight in their original Icelandic texts. His study naturally led him to the Old English poem *Beowulf.* The language of this epic poem was complicated and he could not understand all of it, but he was fascinated by the way it sounded and by the dramatic adventure story it told. He began to perceive the firsthand glimpses of history that were contained within these ancient sto-

ries. He would continue to study *Beowulf* in an attempt to understand it better; though he did not know it at the time, he would one day become one of the world's leading authorities on that important work.

T.C.B.S.

After his separation from Edith, Ronald's primary social circle consisted of other young men his own age. He learned to relish the company of other like-minded men both in school and later in the army. The intense role that male camaraderie began to play in Ronald's life would later manifest itself in *The Hobbit* and *The Lord of the Rings,* much as the journey of a band of male heroes was a traditional part of many ancient myths and stories.

As he learned to read and appreciate great works of ancient literature, he felt the need to share and discuss this interest with his friends. This need, ongoing throughout his life, always resulted in the formation of a "men's club." He belonged to at least six such clubs, but the first was the T.C.B.S. at King Edward's. Originally it was called the Tea Club, as members met during afternoon tea (a daily ritual in turn-of-the-century Britain). Later, the name was changed to the Barrovian Society, after the name of the store where they met. Eventually, it was combined and abbreviated simply as T.C.B.S. This club comprised Ronald Tolkien and three of his close friends: Christopher Wiseman, Rob Gilson, and G.B. Smith. All the members shared an interest in Latin and Greek. However, their other interests were quite varied. Ronald's passion was language and literature; others were more interested in topics

Sigurd the knight slays the dragon Fafnir. As a young man, Tolkien read the stories of Sigurd and Fafnir in their original Icelandic texts.

The Tea Club Barrovian Society

Tolkien's lifelong friend Christopher Wiseman describes their prep school discussion club, the T.C.B.S., in Humphrey Carpenter's biography of Tolkien.

"It started in the summer term, with very great daring. Exams went on for six weeks, and if you were not having an exam you really had nothing to do; so we started having tea in the school library. People used to bring 'subventions': I remember someone brought a tin of fish and we didn't care for it, so up it went on a shelf on top of some books, and stayed there until it was nosed out a long time later! We used to boil a kettle on a spirit-stove; but the great problem was what you were to do with the tea-leaves. Well, the Tea Club often went on after school, and the cleaners would come round with their mops and buckets and brooms, throwing sawdust down and sweeping it all up; so we used to put the tea-leaves in their buckets. Those first teas were in the library cubby-hole. Then, as it was the summer term, we went out and had tea at Barrow's Stores in Corporation Street. In the Tea Room there was a sort of compartment, a table for six between two large settles, quite secluded; and it was known as the Railway Carriage. This became a favourite place for us, and we changed our title to the Barrovian Society, after Barrow's Stores. Later, I was editor of the School Chronicle, and I had to print a list of people who had gained various distinctions; so against the people in the list who were members I put an asterisk, and the bottom of the page by the asterisk it said: 'Also members of the T.C.,B.S., etc.' [no one could figure out] what it stood for!"

such as philosophy, art, mathematics, and poetry. The shared interests and varying perspectives each member brought to the group provided a lively and dynamic forum for discussion of a wide range of topics.

Besides discussion of academic concepts, the young men brought their original compositions to the group for criticism and comment. They motivated and encouraged each other to search within themselves for hidden wells of creativity. After seeing a stage version of *Peter Pan* in 1910, Ronald wrote his first poem for the T.C.B.S., which, not surprisingly, was about elves. This club, and others like it, would provide a necessary sounding board for all of Tolkien's work.

LEAVING THE NEST

Ronald's focus on his studies finally paid off. On his second attempt, he passed the Oxford entrance exams. With a grant from King Edward's and financial assistance from Father Francis, he was able to accept his invitation to Exeter College, one of the many schools composing the Oxford University system.

As a graduation present, Father Francis sent Ronald on a summer trip to Switzerland with some friends. They spent several days hiking through the mountains of the Swiss countryside. At nineteen, Ronald had never seen anything like it. He was awestruck by the landscapes he saw on this trip—one of the few real-life adventures he would ever have—and felt connected to the ancient European myths and languages he had been studying. The trip left a lasting impression on him. Near the end of his vacation he came across a postcard with a reproduction of a painting by the German artist J. Madlener. It was titled *Der Berggeist*, or "The Mountain Spirit." The picture featured a kind-looking old man with a long white beard, a cloak, and a wide-brimmed hat sitting under a tree and talking with a young fawn. Ronald kept this postcard for the rest of his life and later wrote on it, "Origin of Gandalf,"[11] in reference to the wise old wizard he later invented as the primary driver of events in *The Lord of the Rings*.

OXFORD

Like many young people making the difficult adjustment to college life away from home and family, Tolkien said that he initially felt "like a young sparrow kicked out of a high nest."[12] However, he adapted so quickly to Oxford and loved it so much that aside from two brief intervals he would spend the rest of his life in the university town. He felt that Oxford was the first real home he had known since his mother's death.

His lodgings, a small apartment with a bedroom and sitting room, were conveniently at the heart of the Exeter campus. Most students of the day came from upper-class British families and took for granted the "scouts" or servants who customarily waited on undergraduates in their apartments. The unprivileged Tolkien had never experienced such comforts. He quickly began to make friends and joined the rugby team, the debate society, and the essay club. He chose to major in classics, which included the study of Latin, Greek, history, art, and philosophy. It was the equivalent of an American liberal arts degree.

Within a short time, Tolkien had developed a replacement for the T.C.B.S., called the Apolaustics. The meeting agendas were similar to those of his prep school group—reading papers and poetry, discussing literature, and debating any subject brought to the table. The only differences at Oxford were the membership and the fact that these meetings centered around dinners, beer, and pipe smoking instead of afternoon tea.

Like many college freshmen, Tolkien was caught up in the relatively unsupervised activities of staying out late, going to parties, and spending a little more time on

As a student at Oxford University, Tolkien furthered his interest in languages and discovered Finnish, the inspiration for his Elvish languge known as Quenya.

his social life than his studies. With the exception of his treasured language classes, he sometimes skipped lectures altogether. He also found himself attending Catholic mass with less frequency during his first year at school. This upset him greatly, but the call of his college chums was too great to ignore. Fortunately, Tolkien managed to keep from falling too far behind. No matter his other priorities, he always made time to further his exploration of language.

Early in his Oxford days, he gained an extraordinary mentor, Joseph Wright. As one of the world's preeminent philologists, Wright had an understanding and appreciation of language surpassing that of anyone Tolkien had ever met. Wright nurtured Tolkien's love of the Welsh language, encouraging him to study more of it. He had had very little exposure to Welsh since the days of watching his coal trucks roll by. Now he dove into the study of it with a passion. He was soon reacquainted with the way that particular language moved him. The more he learned, the more he loved it. In fact, with all the languages he would go on to study, he maintained that "Welsh always attracted me more than any other language."[13] He would later claim that this fascination influenced his fictional world of Middle Earth, stating that "[the] music of the Welsh comes through in naming mountains and other places."[14]

THE MOST BEAUTIFUL LANGUAGE OF ALL

At King Edward's, Tolkien had come across an ancient Finnish text called the *Kalevala,* a collection of epic stories of heroes, gods, and monsters. He originally read an English translation, but wanted someday to read it in the original Finnish. Then in the library at Exeter he came across a book on the Finnish language that changed not only the way he looked at languages, but his entire future.

Though Welsh was the language that fascinated him the most, he considered Finnish the most lyrical and beautiful language he had ever encountered. In his words, "It was like discovering a wine-cellar filled with bottles of amazing wine of a kind and flavor never tasted before. It quite intoxicated me."[15]

Though he learned only enough Finnish to get through the original text of the *Kalevala,* he was inspired by it to take his language invention to the next level. He gave up his work on Gothic and set out to invent the most beautiful language ever spoken. Based heavily on Finnish, it eventually developed it into a language that would be known as Quenya. Though he did not know it yet, years later this would be the language spoken by the high elves of Middle Earth.

A NEW MAJOR

While his interest in languages continued to grow, Tolkien's attention to his other subjects did not. During his sophomore exams at Oxford, he only received a second class, or roughly the equivalent of a B. However, he received a pure alpha, a nearly perfect score, in one subject: comparative philology. His professors convinced him to change his major from classics to English language and literature at this point, as it was clear that the study of language was his passion.

He was leery of switching to such a restrictive major. Upon seeing his first syllabus, or course description, Tolkien became worried. Already familiar with so much of the material, he could not imagine how this major could keep him busy for another two years. His fears were somewhat realized when he met his first teacher, Kenneth Sisam. Only four years older than Tolkien Sisam initially did not appear to be an expert in the same league as Tolkien's revered Joseph Wright. Over time, however, Tolkien came to appreciate Sisam, and eventually the two collaborated on published works. He quickly found plenty of work to do in his new major. He began to discover and study whole new layers of language, especially in the field of Old and Middle English. Coming across an Old English poem known as *Crist of Cynewulf,* he discovered two lines that captured his imagination:

> Eala Earendel engla beorhtast
> ofer middangeard monnum sended.
>
> Hail Earendel, brightest of angels
> Above the middle-earth sent unto men.[16]

"I felt a curious thrill," he wrote of reading these lines, "as if something had stirred in me, half wakened from sleep. There was something very remote and strange and beautiful behind those words, if I could grasp it, far beyond ancient English."[17] He would continue to ponder these words for many months.

The following summer, while on vacation at his Aunt Jane's farm, he wrote a poem based on these lines called *The Voyage of Earendel the Evening Star.* It told the story of Earendel and his starship voyage of discovery across the heavens. It began:

> Earendel sprang up from the Ocean's cup
> In the gloom of the mid-world's rim;
> From the door of Night as a ray of light
> Leapt over the twilight brim,
> And launching his bark like a silver spark
> From the golden-fading sand
> Down the sunlit breath of Day's fiery death
> He sped from Westerland.[18]

This poem was the first story he ever wrote that would go on to be included in his mythology of Middle Earth.

EDITH RETURNS

When J.R.R. Tolkien woke up on January 3, 1913, he knew exactly what he would be doing that day, his twenty-first birthday. Immediately he began to write a letter to his lost love, Edith Bratt. Though he had spent the years of their separation busy with academics, sports, and his friends, he had never forgotten her. Father Francis's firm edict expired on this day and Tolkien wasted no time.

His letter explained how much he had missed her and asked her how long it

A POWERFUL INFLUENCE

Tolkien had many influences in his life. One of the most profound influences on his study of languages was his Oxford professor Joseph Wright. This excerpt from Michael White's Tolkien biography gives a brief background of the man's humble beginnings and subsequent rise to stardom in the field of linguistics.

"[Joseph Wright] was far removed from the stereotype of the Oxford [professor]. He had been born in a small Yorkshire town and at the age of six had been sent to work in the local woolen mill. He [could not read or write], but by the time he was fifteen he began to realize an entire world lay just beyond his reach—the world of words, language, and writing. He taught himself to read and write and started at night school, where he studied French and German before moving on quickly to Latin. By the age of eighteen, he left the mill and set up his own night school in a spare bedroom in his mother's house. Having earned a little money, he then set out to travel Europe and found his way to Heidelberg, where he earned a degree and then a doctorate. Along the way he mastered Russian, Old Norse, Old Saxon, Old English, and many other languages both contemporary and ancient. Returning to England, Joe Wright set up home in Oxford and was eventually appointed to the position of Deputy Professor of Comparative Philology, a post for which no one could have been better qualified. In 1892 (the year of Tolkien's birth), Wright wrote *A Primer of the Gothic Language*, which Ronald had been given by his teacher at King Edward's."

would be until they could be joined "before God and the world?"[19] When he received her reply just a few days later, he was shocked. Years had passed without communication, and during that time she had moved on and become engaged to another man.

Tolkien was certain that Edith was the love of his life and he refused to take no for an answer. Upon receiving her letter, he immediately boarded a train for Cheltenham, where Edith lived. She met him at the station and they spent the day sitting in a field talking about their lives. By the end of the day, Edith had decided to break off her engagement with the other man and marry her beloved Ronald. Their engagement was not, however, as idyllic as their reunion.

Though Edith was overjoyed to be reunited, she faced complex, serious decisions. Tolkien insisted that she convert to Catholicism, so they could be properly married before God. Edith had become an active member of her church and was reluctant to give up her friends there. Of far greater concern on her part was the reaction of her remaining family, most notably, the uncle with whom she lived. As she suspected, he was outraged at her conversion and threw her out of the house. She moved to Warwick, an area near Birmingham, and shared a place with her cousin Jennie. Ronald and Edith discovered that during the years they had been apart, each had changed and grown. Tolkien's relationship with his studies and his male friends had focused

A SWISS HOLIDAY

After graduation from King Edward's, Tolkien went with his brother on a hiking trip through the Swiss Alps. Tolkien describes his experience, which is often cited as the inspiration for a scene in The Lord of the Rings *in which the fellowship must pass through a dangerous snow-covered mountain pass as they set out toward Mordor. Tolkien's description is quoted in Carpenter's* J.R.R. Tolkien.

"One day we went on a long march with guides up the Aletsch glacier—when I came near to perishing. We had guides but either the effects of the hot summer were beyond their experience, or they did not much care, or we were late in starting. Anyway at noon we were strung out in file along a narrow track with a snow-slope on the right going up to the horizon, and on the left a plunge down into a ravine. The summer of that year had melted away much snow, and stones and boulders were exposed that (I suppose) were normally covered. The heat of the day continued the melting and we were alarmed to see many of them starting to roll down the slope at gathering speed: anything from the size of oranges to large footballs, and a few much larger. They were whizzing across our path and plunging into the ravine. They started slowly, and then usually held a straight line of descent, but the path was rough and one had also to keep an eye on one's feet. I remember the party just in front of me (an elderly schoolmistress) gave a sudden squeak and jumped forward as a large lump of rock shot between us. About a foot at most before [me]."

his interests on subjects that were completely foreign to Edith. She, on the other hand, had become a proper upper-middle-class Englishwoman concerned with daily activities that he found trivial and meaningless.

Though there would always be a deep and profound love between them, they would spend the rest of their lives trying to understand each other and not always succeeding. He would never include her in his circle of friends or his academic pursuits. In fact, in the years prior to their reunion, he had never even mentioned her to the members of the T.C.B.S. or his college friends. Edith had a difficult time adjusting to her lonely life in Warwick while her fiancé wrote her letters about the rollicking good times he was having as an undergraduate at Oxford.

Chapter

3 Off to War

In the summer of 1914, millions of young British men were enlisting in the armed forces, eager to defend their nation in the first World War. Tolkien wanted very much to do his part in the fight against Germany. However, he was also very concerned about completing his studies at Oxford. He felt that he was on track to receive a first class in English language and literature—the equivalent of graduating with high honors. He would need to graduate with this level of distinction if he hoped to go on to a teaching position.

Not wanting to lose his academic momentum, Tolkien decided to finish his final year of school before enlisting. When he returned to Oxford, he found that only one of his friends had come back. The rest were off training for the war. Tolkien was very happy to discover a program at school which gave him some military training while completing his studies. Through this program, he hoped he would be fully prepared to jump into the war as soon as he graduated.

THE LAST GATHERING

The other three members of Tolkien's prep school circle would be shipping off to the war soon and they felt it was important that they spend some time together. So during Christmas break of 1914, the T.C.B.S. met for the last time. They spent a weekend together in London, having a great time sharing stories, thoughts, pipes, and beer. As always, they were a source of inspiration to each other and continued to talk of how, together, they were destined to change the world.

Tolkien would later comment that this Christmas meeting would inspire him to find "a voice for all kind of pent up things."[20] He often spoke of the remarkable inspiration he felt after spending any time with these other young men. At this particular meeting, he came to the firm realization that he had a lot to say. He would never be happy just studying language, but wanted to create with it as well.

Deciding that he was a poet at heart, he began writing about everything he saw. He continued to correspond with the T.C.B.S., sharing his volumes of poetry with them. He was never very happy with much of what he wrote during this time. His poem about Earendel was the thing he loved the most and he continued working on and expanding that. What could be considered his first published work was a short poem titled "Goblin Feet." It was published in a few anthologies, as well as in the annual volume of Oxford poetry. Tolkien claims to have written it for Edith because she enjoyed tales of "spring and flowers and trees, and little elfin people."[21]

A Soldier and a Husband

In June 1915, Tolkien took his final exams and earned his first class honors in English language and literature from Exeter College. Immediately afterward, he enlisted in the army and reported for basic training. He spent nearly a year stationed in England. As a university graduate he was automatically given an officer's commission and required to undergo advanced training. He had no interest in being a platoon leader so he decided to specialize in signaling. It seemed the best use of his natural talent for learning languages.

He learned Morse code, flag, disc, and lamp signaling; heliograph (mirror signaling); signal rockets; and field telephone operation. He even learned to work with carrier pigeons. He was eventually given the post of signaling officer for the Thirteenth Battalion of an army division known as the Lancashire Fusiliers.

Tolkien knew he would soon be shipping out to combat. He and Edith decided they

GOBLIN FEET

One of Tolkien's early attempts at poetry, "Goblin Feet" became his first published work, appearing in Oxford Poetry, *edited by G.D.H. Cole and T.W. Earp, in 1915.*

"I am off down the road
Where the fairy lanterns glowed
And the little pretty flittermice are flying:
A slender band of grey
It runs creepily away
And the hedges and the grasses are a-sighing.

The air is full of wings
Of the blundering beetle-things
That warm you with their whirring.
O! I hear the tiny horns
Of enchanted leprechauns
And the padding feet of many gnomes a-coming.

O! the lights! O! the gleams: O! the little tinkly sounds:
O! the rustle of their noiseless little robes:
O! the echo of their feet, of their little happy feet:
O! their swinging lamps in little star-lit globes."

British soldiers prepare to charge during the Battle of the Somme. The brutality horrified Tolkien.

should be married before he left, as this night may be their last chance to be united as husband and wife. On March 22, 1916, they were married in a small church in Warwick. They took a brief honeymoon in Somerset, a popular English vacation town. When they returned, Edith moved to Straffordshire, so she could be near her new husband's unit. Just two months later, he got his marching orders and shipped off to France.

As an officer, Tolkien was not supposed to socialize with the men in the ranks. However, he had a far greater respect for enlisted men, who put their lives on the line every day, than for many officers. All the officers were assigned privates as their "batmen," or servants. Primarily through this contact, Tolkien did get to know and befriend several enlisted men, and his admiration for them grew. He later acknowledged that one of the characters that would later appear in *The Lord of the Rings* was based on these men: "My 'Sam Gamgee' is indeed a reflection of the English soldier, of the privates and batmen I knew in the 1914 war, and recognised as so far superior to myself."[22]

While Frodo Baggins is the central character in *Lord of the Rings,* more than one critic has argued that Sam Gamgee, Frodo's simple but faithful gardener-turned-servant, is the true protagonist. Certainly, the character is painted in a very brave and noble light, reflecting Tolkien's admiration for the "common" men who are the real heroes of war.

THE BATTLE OF THE SOMME

Tolkien's first encounter with war in France was the Battle of the Somme, remembered as the site of the bloodiest battle ever fought in history. On the first day of the battle, several weeks before Tolkien arrived, more than nineteen thousand British troops were killed. By the time the battle was over, ten months later, more than eight hundred thousand soldiers were dead.

When Tolkien arrived, he was stationed in the nearby town of Bouzincourt, where he waited for his battalion to be sent to the front lines. While waiting, he was met with a most unexpected and pleasant surprise: His fellow T.C.B.S. member G.B. Smith arrived in the town for a brief layover. Smith had already been to the front line of the battle and fortunately returned uninjured. His company had been pulled back to rest before returning to the battle. Over the next few days, the young men talked endlessly about life, poetry, and war. Before long, however, Tolkien's battalion was given their orders. They said good-bye for the last time, and both marched off to battle.

Though the battle had been going on for many weeks, and casualties had been mounting, the Thirteenth Battalion of the Lancashire Fusiliers marched forward with high spirits. They were fighting for the freedom of their country and perhaps the world. In addition, they had been told that the battle was nearly over, as advance troops had surely dismantled the German defenses.

As it turned out, the advance troops had been unsuccessful, and when Tolkien arrived on the field, he was met with a scene he described as pure animal horror. A sea of dead and dying men covered the once beautiful French countryside, which had been stripped bare and replaced with a landscape of mud and trenches and burned, blackened trees. The troops continued to advance, but many of Tolkien's company were killed and the assault did not rout the Germans. Fortunately, Tolkien survived and his troop was sent back to Bouzincourt to recuperate. When he arrived back in camp, he found a letter left there for him by G.B. Smith informing him that their friend Rob Gilson had been killed in battle. The T.C.B.S. was broken.

Over the next three months, Tolkien's battalion alternately advanced into the trenches and retreated to regroup. Each time he entered battle, he grimly faced his own mortality and that of the men around him. Much of his battalion never made it home to England and Tolkien never forgot the horror of what he saw or the bravery of the men who fought alongside him. Many years later, he drew on these memories in his fiction. The blackened landscape of Mordor, home of the evil Sauron, and the Battle of Helm's Deep in *The Two Towers* read as if they came straight from these experiences.

SAVED BY ILLNESS

Trench fever, a disease carried by lice in the unsanitary conditions of the trenches, infected thousands of soldiers, Tolkien among them. Too sick to fight, he was removed from the battlefield and sent to a French hospital to recover. When his fever had not subsided after several weeks, he was sent back to England to recuperate. Trench fever often lingered for a time, and

Tolkien's health had never been robust. So, he spent the next two years in and out of hospitals, trying to combat the fever. Each time he recovered, he would be posted somewhere in England in preparation for a return to the front; again a relapse would send him back to the hospital.

This period of prolonged convalescence kept him off the front lines while the rest of his battalion were either killed or captured. During this time, Edith gave birth to John Francis Reuel Tolkien, the first of the couple's four children, and Tolkien began to create the concept of Middle Earth and the foundations of his epic mythology.

A GREAT MISSION BEGINS

While recovering in England, he received a letter informing him that G.B. Smith had died in battle. Two of his three closest friends were now gone. The T.C.B.S. seemed lost forever. However, just before Smith died, he had written in a letter to Tolkien: "The death of one of its members cannot, I am determined, dissolve the T.C.B.S. Death can make us loathsome and helpless as individuals, but it cannot put an end to the immortal four! . . . May God bless you, my dear John Ronald, and may you say the things I have tried to say long after I am not there to say them, if such be my lot."[23] Tolkien took those words to heart. He believed that, as a group, the T.C.B.S. was meant for great things and the death of one or more of them only meant the burden to fulfill this destiny lay more heavily on the survivors.

With so much free time in the hospital, he decided the moment had come for him

The End of the T.C.B.S.

Tolkien claims to have drawn great inspiration from his first "men's club," known as the T.C.B.S., which met for the last time in London during Christmas 1914. Two of the club's four members were killed in World War I. Upon hearing of the death of Rob Gilson, Tolkien wrote to his fellow members; the letter is reprinted in Humphrey Carpenter's The Letters of J.R.R. Tolkien.

"So far my chief impression is that something has gone crack. . . . I honestly feel that the TCBS has ended—but I am not at all sure that it is not an unreliable feeling that will vanish—like magic perhaps when we come together again. Still I feel a mere individual at present—with intense feelings more than ideas but very powerless.

Of course the TCBS may have been all we dreamt—and its work in the end be done by three or two or one survivor and the part of the others be trusted by God to that of the inspiration which we do know we all got and get from one another. To this I now pin my hopes, and pray God that the people chosen to carry on the TCBS may be no fewer than we three. . . .

I do however dread and grieve about it—apart from my own personal longings—because I cannot abandon yet the hope and ambitions . . . that first became conscious at the Council of London. That Council was as you know followed in my own case with my finding a voice for all kinds of pent up things and a tremendous opening up of everything for me:—I have always laid that to the credit of the inspiration that even a few hours with the four always brought to all of us."

to begin creating something worthy of his lost comrades. Smith had read many of Tolkien's poems over the last two years, since their Christmas meeting. He was a firm critic of much of it, but particularly liked the verse about Earendel, the star mariner. In a letter to Tolkien, he had said that he wanted to know what it was really about. Tolkien wrote back, saying he honestly did not know but he would find out, a response that underscores his beliefs about the origins of his stories.

Tolkien maintained that he did not invent his stories. Instead, he claimed, they were "revealed" to him, as a slice of true history glimpsed through a veil between worlds. As he put it, "[The stories] arose in my mind as 'given' things, and as they came, separately, so too the links grew. . . . Always I had the sense of recording what was already 'there', somewhere: not of 'inventing.'"[24]

Inspired by the death of Smith and his newfound need to create, he began looking for the story behind Earendel. His star mariner had embarked on a great adventure across the heavens and Tolkien was always certain that there was a larger story behind what Earendel had seen.

He was also working furiously on his invented language, Quenya. By this time, Quenya had become quite sophisticated. It had all the elements and intricacies of a true language. He began writing poetry in it as well. As he took this language to the level of creative literature, a familiar question arose. Just as he had always wondered about the people who had spoken the other ancient languages he had studied, he wondered about the people who would have spoken Quenya. There was never a question in his mind that the language had existed—in what might be described as an alternate reality—along with a people to speak it. He felt that the language, like his poetry, was simply revealed to him through divine grace.

THE LOST TALES

Suddenly the veil lifted and it became clear to him that the people who spoke this beautiful language had to be the fairies, or elves, whom Earendel had met on his journeys. From this point forward, Tolkien be-

THE *KALEVALA*

The Kalevala *is an epic poem viewed by the people of Finland as their national mythology. This poem and its creator had a powerful influence on Tolkien and his desire to give his own country a mythological history of its own.*

As Tolkien once explained in a college paper, this so-called ancient Finnish mythology was actually produced less than a hundred years before his own time by a man named Elias Lonnrot. In the 1830s Finland became an independent nation after years of foreign rule. The prolonged subjugation of their culture had virtually erased all records of the history of the Finnish people, so Lonnrot took on the task of piecing it back together. He traveled the country for years, speaking to local villagers and collecting the tales and stories that had been passed down through the centuries by their ancestors. He found many connections among these fantastic stories of heroes, magic, nature, and even gods. When his research was complete, he patched together the stories into a single epic. He introduced his *Kalevala*, or *Land of Heroes*, to the Finnish people and they embraced it as a treasured link to their long-lost identity. Even today, its publication date is a national holiday in Finland.

gan to write a series of poems about Earendel and the elves. The first, called "The Shores of Faery," described Earendel's visit to Valinor, the home of the elves. Here they revealed to the traveler the history and mythology of their world.

He had played around with these stories for some time when Christopher Wiseman, the only other surviving member of the T.C.B.S., wrote to him from France and told Tolkien that it was time he finished his epic. He would always need his friends to push him toward finishing his great works. With a push from Wiseman, he went out and bought a small dime-store notebook and, on its cover, he wrote "The Book of Lost Tales." This notebook would eventually develop into *The Silmarillion,* which chronicles the entire history and mythology of Middle Earth across thousands of years.

Tolkien's obsession with this project was greater than anything he had previously worked on. As he had done in studying Gothic, he decided that Quenya must have an antecedent, upon which it was based. He began piecing together the roots of the Quenyan language and, before long, he had built an entire second language, called Sindarin. While Quenya was based on the lyrical Finnish language, he modeled his new language after his other favorite, Welsh. In typical Tolkien fashion, he proceeded immediately to create a people for Sindarin. These would be a type of lesser elf, who represented an earlier, less lofty version of his high elves. He found that not only was he creating a history for his fictional world, but that he was incorporating elements from the early history of northern Europe. In effect, he was blending reality and fantasy.

A MYTHOLOGY FOR ENGLAND

The concept of mixing history with legend was familiar to him since his exposure several years earlier to the English translation of the collection of epic Norse poetry known as the *Kalevala.* The poem was considered a national treasure in Finland and viewed as the traditional ancient mythology of their country. He was so entranced by the notion of this poem, and the way it transformed the modern Finnish people—giving them a sense of identity and history—that he had written and presented a paper on it at Exeter. When speaking of the *Kalevala,* he once said, "These mythological ballads are full of that very primitive undergrowth that the literature of Europe has on the whole been steadily cutting and reducing for many centuries. . . . I would that we had more of it left—something of the same sort that belonged to the English."[25]

Tolkien was always proud of his cultural roots, but he wished that his own people had a more concrete ancient history. His ancestors were Anglo-Saxons, who had originally come from central Europe to settle in England. Nearly a thousand years ago, the Norman Conquest of England all but wiped out the history of these people. Today, only sparse bits of Anglo-Saxon history exist. These texts, such as *Beowulf,* which describes the fantastic adventures of a sixth-century warrior, had always fascinated Tolkien with the historical insights they provided, but he yearned to know more.

He firmly believed that tradition was the glue that held societies together. Myths are often thought of as a vital link to the roots of a culture. The stories are universal and timeless, providing moral and ethical guideposts for a society to cling to in times of change. Early in his work on the history of Middle Earth, he discovered the great work of his life that he had been searching for. He would attempt to create a unified mythology for his country, similar to the *Kalevala*. He wished to give back to his country the ancient Anglo-Saxon history erased by the Normans.

His Life's Work

Though *The Hobbit* and *The Lord of the Rings* brought him commercial success and enduring fame, Tolkien considered his *Book of Lost Tales* to be the great work of his life. Though he completed a first draft of it by 1925, he continued to perfect it throughout his life. It was not published in its final form—*The Silmarillion*—until several years after his death. His perfectionism was both a curse and a blessing. It kept him from publishing more than a handful of works, but it lent a layer of depth and realism to his work that had never been seen in popular literature before.

His attention to detail was never more evident than in this mythology. He would plan out with great care the names of every character and place in Middle Earth. Each one was layered with hidden meaning, usually decipherable only to a trained philologist. He constructed elaborate family trees and delved painstakingly into the linguistic plausibility of each and every name and pronunciation.

This level of attention also supported his goal of making it a viable mythology for England. As Tolkien put it, "If you want to write a tale of this sort, you must consult your roots."[26] For example, the language and dialects of Rohan, one of the primary nations in the western part of Middle Earth, drew on true medieval history. The unusual and very specific dialect of speech used in Rohan is exactly the same as the Middle English dialect spoken by the inhabitants of Tolkien's own West Midland County many centuries earlier. The Rohannim even refer to their own land as the Mark, the same name that had been used by locals in referring to their West Midland countryside.

Of Beren and Luthien

Tolkien often described one of the stories in *The Book of Lost Tales* as the one he loved most. Not surprisingly, it was based on his deep love for his wife, Edith. After the birth of their first son, Edith moved to Yorkshire to be near her husband's camp. Whenever he could get leave, they would go off into the woods near the camp, where they would sit and talk for hours and she would enchant her husband by singing and dancing for him.

From these encounters came the story that would eventually be titled "Of Beren and Luthien." It was the tale of a mortal man named Beren, who stumbled into an enchanted forest. He encountered a beautiful elf maid, Luthien, who was singing and dancing in the woods. Luthien's beauty was legendary in Middle Earth, and Beren quickly fell in love with her. Despite her father's anger, she ran off with Beren and they began an epic quest of adventure, romance, tragedy, loss, and hope. Not only did this story become a centerpiece of his mythology, as their deeds became central to the history of Middle Earth, but it helped him forever preserve the love he had for his wife. He would often think of her as his Luthien, and of himself as her Beren. In fact, these names would appear beneath their own on the stones that marked their graves many years later.

4 The Professor

Tolkien enjoyed his two years of creative indulgence. Shuffling back and forth between hospitals and army camps gave him an enormous amount of free time to work on his saga of Middle Earth. However, Edith was growing unhappy. She was forced to travel from town to town in order to stay near her husband, unable to establish a home for their young son. She did not enjoy this kind of life and as soon as the war ended in late 1918, Tolkien decided it was time to settle down.

THE OXFORD ENGLISH DICTIONARY

Though he had traveled through England and France, Tolkien's heart had never left Oxford. He had fallen in love with the intellectual life of academia and the community and tradition of Oxford, and he wanted more than anything to spend his career there, studying language and teaching it to others. Unfortunately, jobs were scarce after the war and, despite his exemplary academic record, he was unable to secure a teaching position at the university. Regardless, he moved back to Oxford to take a job offered by one of his old teachers that seemed perfect for him.

Sir James Murray had begun work on *The Oxford English Dictionary*, popularly called the *OED*, in 1878 and intended it to be the world's first comprehensive dictionary of the English language. Originally, he thought it would take ten years to complete the project, but five years into it his staff had only reached the word *ant*. Not until 1900 was the first volume (A–H) published. Further installments were released at regular intervals but the dictionary was not completed until 1928, long after Murray had died. Murray's four chief editors took over the project after his death. One of these men, W.A. Craigie, had been Tolkien's professor of Icelandic studies. Very impressed with the young student's work, Craigie offered him a job at the dictionary. The work was detailed and meticulous, a perfect job for a perfectionist like Tolkien. He spent the first few months on the job researching only five words: *worm*, *wasp*, *water*, *wick*, and *winter*. Tolkien took the work very seriously. His entry on *wasp*, for example, included references to thirteen languages.

Tolkien worked on the *OED* for two years, delving into the mysteries of language.

Sir James Murray began work on The Oxford English Dictionary *in 1878, a project that took fifty years to complete.*

He thoroughly enjoyed his work and felt that he learned more during his time there than during any equal period of his life.

His employers were also very happy with his work. The chief editor of the dictionary, Dr. Henry Bradley, said, "His work gives evidence of an unusually thorough mastery of Anglo-Saxon and of the facts and principles of the comparative grammar of the Germanic languages. Indeed, I have no hesitation in saying that I have never known a man of his age who was in these respects his equal."[27] High praise indeed from someone in contact with most of the great philological minds of the century. Tolkien would continue to amaze people with his academic prowess througout his career.

Though J.R.R. Tolkien would go on to write one of the most popular novels of the twentieth century, he spent most of his life struggling to make ends meet for himself and his growing family. Edith was now pregnant with their second child and his paycheck from the dictionary was not enough. In addition, he was still working toward his goal of teaching at Oxford. So, he took on a second job as a tutor of local undergraduates.

Aspiring Oxford professors routinely turned to work as a tutor. This was a contract job and the tutors were paid on a per student basis. Tolkien began tutoring undergraduates at Oxford while working at the dictionary, and found he was well suited for the job, as he had a great passion for sharing his knowledge.

LANGUAGE AND LITERATURE

In J.R.R. Tolkien: Author of the Century, *Tom Shippey, a philology professor at Oxford during Tolkien's time there, explains Tolkien's feelings (which he shared) on the importance of blending the studies of language and literature.*

"Philology is not and should not be confined to language study. The texts in which these old forms of the language survive are often literary works of great power and distinctiveness, and (in the philological view) any literary study which ignores them, which refuses to pay the necessary linguistic toll to be able to read them, is accordingly incomplete and impoverished. Conversely, of course, any study which remains solely linguistic (as was often the case with twentieth-century philology) is throwing away its best material and its best argument for existence. In philology, *literary and linguistic study are indissoluble.* They ought to be the same thing. Tolkien said exactly that in his letter of application to the Oxford Chair in 1925."

LEEDS

In 1919, Tolkien received his master of arts degree, an honorary degree in the Oxford system typically given to postgraduate students who had put in a fair amount of time working with the senior faculty. One year later, he applied for a position as a "reader", or lecturer, in English language at Leeds University in northern England. Despite his own fears that he was too young for such a position, he got the job.

He did not want to leave Oxford, but this opportunity was too good to pass up. The English Department at Leeds was small but growing. George Gordon, the professor who had hired Tolkien, had recently decided to reshape the department. He wanted it to mimic Oxford's English Department by giving the students a choice of two focuses: pre-Chaucerian English or post-Chaucerian English. Oxford's English program was called English Language and Literature because some students chose the era before Chaucer's *Canterbury Tales* (ca. A.D. 1400) and were considered students primarily of language. They were interested in piecing together the linguistic fragments of this time, as a way of unlocking the mysteries of English. Other students who chose to study post-Chaucerian English were more interested in studying the plentiful body of literature that existed in more modern times, as a way of learning about the language. In theory this system provided the students with a well-rounded approach to the study of English. In practice, most students and readers fell firmly into one camp or the other and spent very little time focusing on the other perspective.

A NEW BRAND OF ENGLISH

Tolkien's task was to create a syllabus, or course outline, at Leeds that would provide a solid grounding in philology and still be enticing to undergraduates who wanted to read modern literature. The challenge excited him and he took it eagerly. It was not easy for him at first, as the students at Leeds were very different from those at Oxford. Oxford, the crown jewel of the English university system, attracted a very high caliber of student; Leeds was a much smaller school and attracted many local Yorkshire residents.

Tolkien made the transition, and he did such a remarkable job redesigning the English curriculum at Leeds that during his first year there, he received an invitation to apply to two other universities. One of them, DeBeers University in South Africa, offered him a position. He had always wanted to go back to the land of his birth, but because Edith was adamantly opposed, he turned down the post and remained at Leeds.

E.V. GORDON

Though he would always question how his life would have been different had he taken the position at DeBeers, he was very happy to remain at Leeds. In 1922, Leeds hired E.V. Gordon, one of the Oxford students Tolkien had tutored, as a reader, and his arrival enriched Tolkien's life at Leeds.

Tolkien was always happiest when in the company of good friends and Gordon became an important figure in his life.

Though he had been Tolkien's student, his knowledge of Welsh far exceeded that of any other faculty member, including Tolkien himself. They learned a great deal from each other.

Shortly after Gordon arrived, the two men created a reading club for the undergraduates. Called the Viking Club, it was a place where the students could join the two professors to drink beer, read epic poetry, and sing comic songs. Tolkien and Gordon wrote most of the humorous poems and songs, which often poked fun at the students and other faculty, in Old English or Icelandic. This club made the two readers quite popular with the young students. Combined with their scholarly achievements, passionate lecturing, and enthusiastic nurturing of the students, the Viking Club helped to transform the English Department at Leeds.

By 1925, more than a third of the English majors were enrolled in the newly created Language concentration. This was actually a much higher percentage than the split seen at Oxford.

PUBLISHING

The expression "publish or perish" is often used in academic circles to mean that a professor's career depends more on his or her record of published work than on demonstrated teaching skills. Tolkien always struggled with this mandate as his perfectionism kept him from finishing many of the works he began. However, he started off very well. His old tutor at Oxford, Kenneth Sisam, had written a book on Middle English and asked Tolkien to create a vocabulary for it, as he had such a profound grasp of the language. The project gained Tolkien considerable notice in the field. His second project, however, was to be far more important.

One of the Middle English texts he had studied since high school had always held a special fascination for him. *Sir Gawain and the Green Knight* is the Arthurian tale of a knight who takes a bet that will mean his own death, in an effort to protect his king. Because only fragments of the story remained completely intact, anyone wishing to study the complete work in its original Middle English had to consult a number of different sources. Tolkien and Gordon collaborated on a project to edit and compile a complete version of the ancient story. Their work was eventually published by the Oxford University Press in 1925 and is still used today in universities as the standard edition of the Middle English text.

THE YOUNG PROFESSOR

Tolkien continued to study language and to inspire others to do the same. He taught a two-year course on another of his favorite Anglo-Saxon works, the Old English epic *Beowulf*. Though opinions varied on his skill as a lecturer, many students marveled at the way he brought life to these dead stories. One young girl recalled the opening lecture in his *Beowulf* series and said,

> He came in lightfully and gracefully, I always remember that, his gown flowing, his fair hair shining, and he read Beowulf aloud. We did not know the

Beowulf battles the monster Grendel. Tolkien taught a two-year course on Beowolf *during his time at Leeds University.*

LEADING LEWIS TO CHRISTIANITY

J.R.R. Tolkien and C.S. Lewis were both very religious men, but Tolkien's influence on Lewis's beliefs was the stronger. Though raised a Protestant, C.S. Lewis had rejected Christianity early in life. He firmly believed in the power of myth to guide the morals of a society, but he did not view religion as more than myth or the Bible as more than mythological literature. Tolkien, on the other hand, was a devout Christian and his belief in God was unshakable. The two men spent many hours discussing their religious philosophies.

On one of their evening strolls, Tolkien managed to break through to his friend. He convinced Lewis that viewing the story of Christ as a myth is not incompatible with belief in Christ as the son of God. This was a turning point for Lewis, who had not found a way to accept Christianity until Tolkien provided the insight. From this point forward, Lewis became an increasingly religious man. Later in life, he would go on to write a number of powerful books about God and the Christian spirit. Tolkien recorded their conversation that night in the form a poem he would later publish, titled "Mythopoeia." One of his lesser-known works, "Mythopoeia" summarizes many of Tolkien's feelings on the relation between mythology and modern religion.

language he was reading, yet the sound of Tolkien made sense of the unknown tongue and the terrors and the dangers that he recounted—how I do not know—made our hair stand on end. He read like no one else I have ever heard. . . . He was a great teacher, and delightful, courteous, ever so kindly.[28]

Crossword puzzles had just become a popular fad in the early 1920s, so Tolkien created his own Anglo-Saxon versions of them for his students. During his time at Leeds, he was often described as an open and friendly lecturer. His success led the university to create a new position for him. In the English University system, each department has a number of lecturers but only one professor, or chairman. At the age of 32, Tolkien became the youngest professor at Leeds when he was placed in charge of the newly created department of the English Language.

Opportunity Knocks

Tolkien's third child, Christopher Reuel, was born the same year he was raised to professor. He was becoming quite settled into his life at Leeds, but it did not last long. After just one year as a new professor, he learned of an opening at Oxford. Although the competition for professorship at Oxford was very stiff and he was still very young, he applied immediately. Due in part to his work on *Sir Gawain and the Green Knight,* he was given the post of professor of Anglo-Saxon at Oxford's Bosworth and Rawlinson College. Elated, he and his family moved back to Oxford. This time, he was home for good. He would not leave Oxford again for more than forty years.

Though he was thrilled to be back, he was dismayed by the ways Oxford had begun to change. Woods were being cleared for housing, and the commercial center of Oxford began to look more like a city than a quiet English village. Over the years Tolkien lived there, the city would continue to expand, absorbing suburbs, and whittling away the fields and woods in the surrounding countryside to make way for new homes, roads, and shopping plazas. Automobiles were also becoming more popular. Tolkien abhorred them, only owning one for a very brief period of his life. He felt that they polluted the air, and the roads created for them were destroying the countryside.

C.S. Lewis

Tolkien never tolerated change well and the way Oxford was changing made him withdraw a bit from society. Though he remained a relatively good-natured person, he became more reserved and selective about the company he kept, after his return to Oxford. Fortunately, he met someone who shared many of his attitudes and beliefs. His name was C.S. Lewis.

Lewis was a tutor in the English Department at Oxford's Magdalen College, and he would later become famous for writing a number of books on religion and fantasy, including the seven-volume *Chronicles of Narnia.* The two men formed an intense friendship that would last over the next forty years. They were kindred souls, both possessing a deep love for Oxford, history, language, mythology, epic poetry, drinking beer, smoking pipes, and talking. Though Lewis was probably the single most influential person in Tolkien's life, their relationship would have its ups and downs. In fact, it nearly ended before it began.

After their first meeting, Lewis described Tolkien in a diary entry, "No harm in him: only needs a smack or so."[29] Their first meeting had been somewhat charged with antagonism, as they found themselves on opposing sides of an issue then being debated in the English Department. When Tolkien returned to Oxford, he found that the split between the language and literature sides of the department had grown out of control. Most members of the faculty were solidly in one camp or the other and constantly fought to have their side more heavily represented in the school's curriculum. Though Tolkien was more of a language person, he argued strongly to have the two sides more integrated. He did not believe that either was complete without the other. He referenced this notion in his letter of application to the post he currently held, saying that his goal was "to advance, to the best of my ability, the . . . neighbourliness of linguistic and literary studies, which can never be enemies except by misunderstanding or without loss to both; and to continue in a wider and more fertile field the encouragement of philological enthusiasm among the young."[30]

Tolkien would work tirelessly over the next decades to bring the two sides together. Because his position as professor lent him no administrative authority at Oxford, change of this sort could only be accomplished through persuasion. In an effort to bring light to the way these two branches of English could enhance each other, he created yet another club. This one, known as the Kolbitars, or Coalbiters, was created as a forum to read and discuss Old Norse epics. The name came from the image of a group of men crowded so closely around a reading fire, that they were "biting the coals."

Originally formed by Tolkien and his young protégé Nevill Coghill, it enticed faculty from both camps. The ones who studied the mechanics of Icelandic language would join to show off their mastery of the ancient tongue. The ones who were more interested in literature would come to hear the epic sagas that they could not read on their own. It proved to be a very popular club and helped unify the department.

Initially, Lewis was not interested in joining the group, as he was wary of Tolkien.

As Lewis recalled, "At my first coming into the world I had been . . . warned never to trust a Papist [a Catholic person], and at my first coming into the English Faculty . . . never to trust a philologist. Tolkien was both."[31] Joining the Coalbiters and befriending Tolkien helped break Lewis of both these prejudices.

TOLKIEN AT HOME

For the first five to six years of their friendship, Tolkien and Lewis spent an enormous amount of time together. They discussed every topic imaginable and presented their work to the other for criticism. And they were often each other's toughest critic.

This camaraderie was not as well appreciated by Tolkien's wife. Edith became jealous of the time they spent together. She had little in common with the other professors' wives and spent nearly all of her time at home with the children, or by herself. By this time, she was busy caring for their fourth and final child, Priscilla. Edith felt that she got very little of her husband's attention and, for most of their married life, she was resentful of the way he distanced her from his academic pursuits and his friends. Tolkien's profound love for his wife would remain throughout his life, but during these years, he found himself so busy that he had little time to devote to any one thing, including her.

He saw his family in the morning before school and again in the evening for a few hours. However, the rest of his day was consumed by his work and his friends. He taught all day, and ate dinner several nights each week at the faculty common rooms, as was expected of an Oxford professor. His lunches were spent with his friends at the local pub. He made some time each night when he came home to spend with his family, but after the children had gone to sleep, he began grading papers and preparing the next day's lectures. He was meticulous about his school work and was as much a perfectionist in this as anything else in life. For example, as a professor, he was required to teach a minimum of thirty-six lectures each year, but he often taught more than a hundred, as he felt there was simply too much knowledge to leave unshared. In addition, he would not lecture unless he had every note of it spelled out and organized (though he would often go completely off topic in the lecture and ramble about unrelated topics

A Son's Memories

In J.R.R. Tolkien: Architect of Middle Earth, *Daniel Grotta includes a letter from Tolkien's son Michael fondly recalling the way his father interacted with him as a child.*

"My earliest memories of him—I am his second son, and was born in Oxford in 1920—was of a unique adult, the only grown-up who appeared to take my childish comments and question with complete seriousness. Whatever interested me seemed invariably to interest him more, even my earliest efforts to talk. Not many years ago he showed me a battered notebook in which he had carefully set down the words I applied to every object I saw.

. . . His bedtime stories seemed exceptional. Unlike other people, he did not read them from a book, but simply told them, and they were infinitely more exciting and much funnier than anything read from the children's books at the time. That quality of reality, of being inside a story and so being a part of it, which has been, I believe, at least an important factor contributing to the worldwide success of his imaginative works, was already apparent to a small, though already critical and fairly imaginative boy. Inevitably, he was not a super-human father, and often he found his children insufferably irritating, self-opinionated, foolish and even occasionally totally incomprehensible. But he never lost his ability to talk *to* and not *at* or *down to* his children. In my own case he always made me feel that what *I* was doing and what *I* was thinking in my youth were of far more immediate importance than anything *he* was doing or thinking."

for lengthy periods). The late hours he kept, while working on these lectures, meant that he and Edith had to keep separate bedrooms, as he did not want to disturb her with his work.

In addition to managing the busy duties of a university professor and a father of four, Tolkien took on part-time jobs grading exam papers for students seeking entrance to Ox-ford. He despised this work as it took him away from more important matters, but he was always in need of extra money to support his family. Last in the list of priorities, but still first in his heart, was his epic work on the mythology of Middle Earth. He never stopped working on it, but found little time to edit the thousands of pages of poems and stories he had already written.

5 The Inklings

Tolkien's mythology for England grew to epic proportions. He had spent so much time writing and rewriting the stories—by hand—that he scarcely knew which stacks of paper contained the oldest versions and which contained the most recently revised versions. He changed the epic saga's name from *The Book of Lost Tales* to *The Silmarillion*, the title under which it would be published more than sixty years after its inception. The name is derived from the three mystic gems at the heart of the story. These gems, known as the Silmarils, embody the light source of heaven and represent the greatest works of the elves of Middle Earth. The gems come to represent the hubris, or pride, of the elves and lead to their expulsion from this heaven, known as Valinor. The quest to recover the lost Silmarils shapes the future of the land and all the races of good and evil in Middle Earth, setting the stage for the events, many thousands of years later, in *The Hobbit* and *The Lord of the Rings*.

THE NEVER-ENDING STORY

Tolkien's greatest desire was to create a mythology for England, but he spent the rest of his life rewriting and revising it.

Why, then, did he never finish it? Tolkien himself never answered the question, but three possible reasons have been proposed by his friends and family. As a perfectionist, he was simply never happy with his work. He felt the need to continue fine-tuning it every time he looked at it, or even thought about it. He also feared rejection. He did not handle rejection very well and, as this was the work of his life, he could not bear the possibility that publishers might slam their doors on the project.

Finally, Tolkien took such great joy in working on these stories and creating the world in which they took place that it is quite possible he simply did not want to end it. He would later write a famous paper on the creation of fantasy literature and would refer to this as a powerful human drive toward "sub-creation."[32] As his good friend Christopher Wiseman wrote to him, "Why these creatures live to you is because you are still creating them. When you have finished creating them, they will be as dead to you as the atoms that make our living food."[33]

THE CLUB TO END ALL CLUBS

For many years, Tolkien had shared his mythology only with his family and with

C.S. Lewis, but in the mid-1930s he found a new forum in which to share his work. By this time, the Coalbiters had managed to read through all the existing Icelandic texts and stopped meeting on a regular basis. Tolkien was never complete unless he was part of a club, so he and Lewis created the Inklings. They borrowed the name from an undergraduate club they had both attended with their students the previous year. After the students stopped attending the meetings, Lewis and Tolkien began inviting their own friends to join.

A very unofficial club, by Oxford standards, the Inklings comprised an ever-changing cast of professors, tutors, and nonacademics such as Lewis's brother, and even the local doctor. They would meet once or twice a week, either in a pub called the Eagle and Child (which they all referred to as the Bird and Baby), or in Lewis's apartment. Though members came

In the mid-1930s, C.S. Lewis (pictured) and J.R.R. Tolkien formed a literary club called the Inklings.

and went over the years, Lewis and Tolkien remained at the heart of the club and would continue to attend the meetings regularly for the next thirty years.

The Inklings became Tolkien's home away from home and the sounding board for all the work he would create during the rest of his life. It often reminded him of his cherished days with the T.C.B.S., as many of the members became good friends and would meet to discuss, as Lewis put it, everything "from beer to Beowulf."[34]

While the discussion was indeed far-ranging, the primary focus of the group was to read and discuss literature. Each meeting began with the booming voice of Lewis proclaiming, "Well, has nobody got anything to read us?"[35] Works of classic literature were sometimes read, but more often it was a forum for its members to read their original works aloud. Following Inkling customs, the men sat back with their pipes and beer, listened intently to the recitation of the week, and then jumped in with immediate criticism. Some of the feedback was quite positive and often encouraging. However, blunt honesty was always the rule; when someone disapproved, he said so. In such cases, weaknesses were analyzed and possible remedies suggested.

Tolkien read much of his work on *The Silmarillion* to the group, as well as anything else he was working on at the time. Most of his work was well received by the group, but when the criticism began to fly, he rarely took the advice that was offered. In fact, C.S. Lewis recalled that Tolkien had only two reactions to criticism: "Either he begins the whole work over again

from the beginning or else takes no notice at all."[36]

THE GENTLEMEN'S AGREEMENT

Neither Tolkien nor Lewis enjoyed reading newspapers or the popular fiction of the day. Both claimed they could find all the excitement and stimulation they needed in classic literature. One day, while discussing the lack of high-quality modern fiction in the world, they decided they would have to write some themselves to fill the void.

Both men had been writing poetry and heroic epics for many years, but neither had ever tried his hand at popular fiction. They decided that each would attempt to write a story; Lewis's would focus on space travel and Tolkien's on time travel. Both stories would involve the discovery of some kind of mythology, real or imagined.

Lewis quickly produced a book called *Out of the Silent Planet*, which he would later publish as the first book in his successful *Ransom* trilogy. Tolkien, on the other hand, went about his normal routine of spending an enormous amount of time and energy on a project that was never published. He attempted to incorporate his Middle Earth mythology into the story by centering it on a father and son who traveled back in time to an ancient pseudo-England and learned about an ancient race of wise and powerful men from a doomed island known as Numenor. Numenor had become the outlet for Tolkien's Atlantis dreams and was eventually incorporated into both *The Silmarillion* and *The Lord of the*

TEARING DOWN THE TOWER

In 1936 Tolkien delivered a lecture at the British Academy on the Anglo-Saxon text Beowulf, *which helped to establish him as one of the world's foremost authorities on the Old English poem. Though he detested the implication of allegory in his fictional works, he did create this allegorical story for his lecture to illustrate his point that students of language had spent so much time picking apart the pieces of* Beowulf *that they were missing the importance of the story itself.*

"A man inherited a field in which was an accumulation of old stone, part of an older hall. Of the old stone some had already been used in building the house in which he actually lived, not far from the old house of his fathers. Of the rest he took some and built a tower. But his friends coming perceived at once (without troubling to climb the steps) that these stones had formerly belonged to a more ancient building. So they pushed the tower over, with no little labour, in order to look for hidden carvings and inscriptions, or to discover whence the man's distant forefathers had obtained their building material. Some suspecting a deposit of coal under the soil began to dig for it, and forgot even the stones. They all said: 'This tower is most interesting.' But they also said (after pushing it over): 'What at a muddle it is in!' And even the man's descendants, who might have been expected to consider what he had been about, were heard to murmur: 'He is such an odd fellow! Imagine his using these old stones just to build a nonsensical tower! Why did not he restore the old house? He had no sense of proportion.' But from the top of that tower the man had been able to look out upon the sea."

Rings, but this particular story, called *The Lost Road*, was left unfinished.

THE STORYTELLER

Though *The Lost Road* was Tolkien's first attempt at popular fiction, he had been creating fanciful stories for quite some time. While many fathers today read bedtime stories to their children, it was a custom in Victorian England for fathers to create these stories themselves. Being a traditionalist, Tolkien revived this custom and would regularly spin yarns for his four children.

For his first son, John, he made up a story about a boy named Carrots. Carrots had bright red hair and would climb into the family's cuckoo clock to have grand adventures. To console son Michael, who had lost his favorite stuffed dog at the beach on summer vacation, his father created "Roverandom," a tale about a small dog that annoyed a wizard, was turned into a toy, and then was lost on the beach. Later, the dog was found by another wizard who reanimated it and then sent it on fantastic adventures on the moon.

"Mr. Bliss" was the story of a tall thin man who lived in a tall thin house, bought a bright yellow car for five shillings, and took it on many extraordinary journeys. A later story was based on another favorite family doll, known as Tom Bombadil. Tom was a wood sprite of sorts and lived as a human extension of the land. "The Adventures of Tom Bombadil" was published in the *Oxford Magazine* in 1934, and the character Tom Bombadil would later appear in *The Lord of the Rings*.

Tolkien attempted to publish several of his stories, and drew some publishers' interest in a few of them. He had illustrated "Mr. Bliss," which one publisher considered as a storybook for very young children. Unfortunately, Tolkien never got around to revising the illustrations to his satisfaction and the story remained unpublished in his lifetime.

Many years later, in light of the success of his major works, he was able to publish several of these stories, including "Roverandom," and a novella called *Farmer Giles of Ham*. After his death, his children went on to publish a number of his stories, such as "Mr. Bliss." They also released a collection of letters he had written them at Christmas, pretending to be Santa Claus. Each year *The Father Christmas Letters* updated the children on St. Nick's supposed adventures at the North Pole and included a host of fun characters, such as his polar bear roommate, his elvish secretary, and

even some nasty goblins that lived beneath the house.

IN A HOLE IN THE GROUND

One evening in his study, Tolkien was suffering through the loathsome task of grading entrance exams for extra cash. He came across a test that had been left blank and stared at it gratefully. After musing over the blank page for a few minutes, he wrote on it the words "In a hole in the ground, there lived a hobbit."[37] He stared at it for a while and realized that he had no idea what a hobbit was. He decided that he had better find out.

Of course, names and strange words always created stories in his mind, and before long—though his children disagree on exactly when—he had begun to tell them a story about a strange little creature named Bilbo Baggins. Though he claims to have pulled the word *hobbit* from the ether, the idealized world they lived in was clearly influenced very heavily by Tolkien's own ideas of paradise. Hobbits live a very simple country life, unconcerned with the affairs of the world beyond their own gardens. Tolkien would later state, "Hobbits are just rustic English people, made small in size because it reflects the generally small reach of their imagination—not the small reach of their courage or latent power."[38]

Not only did the hobbits' home, known as the Shire, reflect many facets of Tolkien's childhood in Sarehole, but the character of Bilbo himself is often called a reflection of the man who created him. Bilbo lives in a house called Bag-End, which is the name

J.R.R. Tolkien modeled hobbits after English country people, the Shire after his childhood home, and Bilbo Baggins after himself.

of the farm belonging to Tolkien's Aunt Jane. He enjoys smoking pipes, drinking ale, and eating plain foods, much like the professor. He is the same age as Tolkien (at the time of writing), and he even struggles through the rest of his long hobbit-life trying to write a great adventure story about dragons and elves. Though Tolkien was always very secretive about the origins and meanings behind many of his characters and stories, he admitted later in life, "I am a hobbit in all but size."[39]

The story of Bilbo's great adventure, eventually published as *The Hobbit*, is rich with trolls, goblins, elves, and even a dragon guarding a horde of treasure. In 1932, Tolkien showed an incomplete first draft of the manuscript to Lewis and read it to the Inklings. Everyone who heard it loved it, and all encouraged Tolkien to finish the manuscript and submit it for publication. Unfortunately, his work at Oxford kept him from finding the time. So, the story went into a drawer, where it sat for the next several years.

THE FATHER CHRISTMAS LETTERS

Each year at Christmas, Tolkien would write letters to his children in the guise of Father Christmas. Biographer Humphrey Carpenter describes these letters and the way in which Tolkien convinced his children of their authenticity.

"Tolkien's talents as a storyteller and an illustrator were combined each December, when a letter would arrive for the children from Father Christmas. In 1920 . . . Tolkien had written a note to his son in shaky handwriting signed 'Yr loving Fr. Chr.'. From then onwards he produced a similar letter every Christmas. From simple beginnings the 'Father Christmas Letters' expanded to include many additional characters such as the Polar Bear who shares Father Christmas's house, the Snow Man who is Father Christmas's gardener, an elf named Ilbereth who is his secretary, snow-elves, gnomes, and in the caves beneath Father Christmas's house a host of troublesome goblins. Every Christmas, often at the last minute, Tolkien would write out an account of recent events at the North Pole in the shaky handwriting of Father Christmas, the [old-fashioned] capitals used by the Polar Bear, or the flowing script of Ilbereth. Then he would add drawings, write the address on the envelope (labeling it with such super-scriptions as 'By gnome-carrier. Immediate haste!') and paint and cut out a highly realistic North Polar postage stamp. Finally he would deliver the letter. This was done in a variety of ways. The simplest was to leave it in the fireplace as if it had been brought down the chimney, and to cause strange noises to be heard in the early morning, which together with a snowy footprint on the carpet in-dicated that Father Christmas himself had called. Later the local postman became an accomplice and used to de-liver the letters himself, so how could the children not be-lieve in them? Indeed they went on believing until each in turn reached adolescence and discovered by accident or deduction that their father was the true author of the letters. Even then, nothing was said to destroy the illu-sion for the younger children."

The Influential Professor

By this time Tolkien had become a well-known and somewhat eccentric figure at the university. One Halloween, he dressed up as a barbarian and was seen chasing people through the streets. According to contemporaries he was a very popular professor at Oxford, much as he had been at Leeds, widely known for his ability to "turn a lecture room into a mead hall [medieval banquet setting] in which he was the bard and [the students] were the feasting, listening guests."[40]

However, some students found his unusual manner of speech difficult to understand or follow. Even many who knew him well commented on his strange accent and rapid, often garbled speech. His diction was not helped by the pipe always clenched between his teeth. Tolkien claimed that his speech impediment was due to a prep school rugby injury in which he severely injured his tongue. However, those who knew him in prep school note that his speech was poor before the accident.

Tolkien also had a tendency to ramble off topic and speak at length on esoteric subjects that had little or no connection to the subject at hand. Some found this habit most annoying, but others considered it part of his enigmatic charm. A colleague once referred to Tolkien as an "inspired speaker of footnotes."[41] Indeed these offhand ramblings were often the most insightful parts of his lectures.

While people debated his lecturing style, most students seemed to agree that his greatest success as a professor was his ability to inspire others. Tolkien's profound passion for language and literature was simply contagious. Though philology was at that time a dying art, Tolkien managed to awaken an interest in it in virtually anyone. Biographer Daniel Grotta comments that

> He gave of his time and knowledge, and strove to impart a love of language and lore to those who previously had only a slight appreciation. To argue that Tolkien helped train an entire generation of English philologists seems scarcely an exaggeration when one considers the number and the quality of his students who chose philology as their profession.[42]

Beowulf

Tolkien's influence extended beyond his students to the faculty of Oxford's English Department. He worked for many years to mend the rift in the English curriculum between language and literature. Through his passion, his academic clubs, and his lectures, he eventually succeeded in his task, and the course requirements changed to reflect a more integrated approach to the study of English, acknowledging both words' history and words' purpose. In describing Tolkien's gift for both aspects of language, C.S. Lewis once wrote of Tolkien that he had a "unique insight at once into the language of poetry and into the poetry of language."[43]

In 1936 Tolkien's passion for this subject helped him to produce one of the most notable works of his academic career. He was asked to deliver a lecture on *Beowulf*, the Old English epic to which he had devoted years of study, to the British Academy. Tolkien had a special love for this heroic poem, the story of a brave knight who must slay a dangerous beast.

One of the oldest and most intact works of Old English, *Beowulf* has been studied and dissected by generations of scholars. Tolkien's lecture brought together the work of these scholars as well as his own philological insights into the Old English language. Most importantly, though, he discussed his concern that linguists had spent so much time picking apart the language of the poem that they were destroying the importance of the story itself. Though he disliked having people look for allegorical meaning in his fiction, he used his storytelling abilities, in this case, to make his point.

He told a story of a man who built a grand tower with some old stones. The man's friends marveled at the tower, then decided to knock it down and pick through the rubble to learn more about the stones. Tolkien pleaded with his audience to enjoy the "tower" of *Beowulf* and learn from it as a whole, not just from its constituent parts. His lecture demonstrated a unique mastery and understanding of the work. As "Beowulf: The Monsters and the Critics," it was published in 1937 and permanently established him as one of the world's leading authorities on the poem.

THE FIRST REVIEW

Several years after Tolkien stopped work on *The Hobbit,* he allowed a friend and former student, Elaine Griffiths, to read the

---

THE MOST IMPORTANT REVIEW

As described in Susan Ang's Master of the Rings, *when Tolkien offered his original manuscript of the* The Hobbit *to publisher Allen and Unwin, it was handed over to the publisher's ten-year-old son, Rayner Unwin, who earned a shilling for writing the following review.*

"Bilbo Baggins was a hobbit who lived in his hobbit-hole and never went for adventures, at last Gandalf the wizard and his dwarves perswaded him to go. He had a very exiting time fighting goblins and wargs. At last they got to the lonley mountain; Smaug, the dragon who gawreds it is killed and after a terrific battle with the goblins he returned home—rich! This book, with the help of maps, does not need any illustrations it is good and should appeal to all children between the ages of 5 and 9."

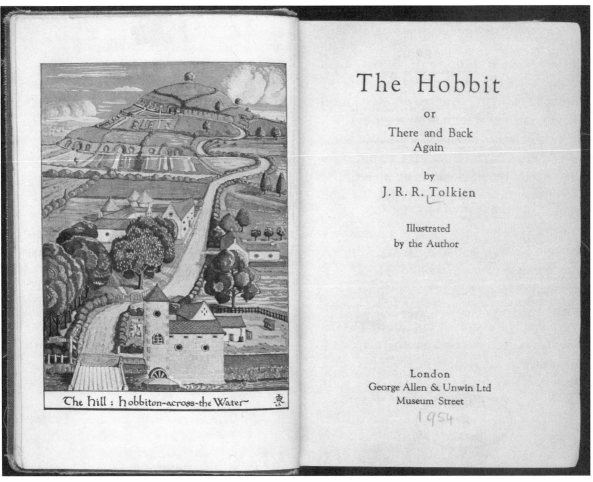

The Hobbit

or

There and Back
Again

by
J. R. R. Tolkien

Illustrated
by the Author

London
George Allen & Unwin Ltd
Museum Street

1954

The hill : hobbiton-across-the-Water

The Hobbit *was first published in 1937. The title page from an early printing shows Tolkien's own illustration of the town of Hobbiton.*

incomplete manuscript. She loved it and, like his other friends, tried to convince him to publish it. Still he hesitated, saying it needed more work. He was also apprehensive that his fellow scholars at Oxford would ridicule him for writing a children's book.

Griffiths gave the manuscript to a friend, Susan Dagnall, an editor at the London publishing house of Allen and Unwin. Dagnall too was captivated. While on business in Oxford, she met Tolkien to plead

with him to complete the manuscript, refusing to take no for an answer. He finally agreed and just a few months later (the fastest he would ever complete work for a publisher), he sent the finished manuscript to Allen and Unwin.

Publisher Stanley Unwin firmly believed that children were the best judges of children's stories, so he gave Tolkien's story to his ten-year-old son, Rayner. Earning one shilling for a written report on the book, Rayner reported that it would "appeal to all children."[44] His father agreed and accepted the book for publication.

THE HOBBIT

Tolkien had become a skillful illustrator over the years, often enhancing his stories with charming drawings and watercolors. Deciding that the book would need illustrations, Allen and Unwin asked him to submit the ones he had created for *The Hobbit,* mostly depictions of the landscapes he describes in the story. He considered his artistic talent too modest for publication, but he allowed Unwin to see the drawings, and the publisher loved them. *The Hobbit* was released with the author's illustrations on September 21, 1937.

Popular and critical acclaim was immediate and overwhelming. One reviewer wrote, "All who love that kind of children's book which can be read and re-read by adults should take note that a new star has appeared in this constellation."[45] In the United States, the New York *Herald Tribune* named *The Hobbit* best juvenile book of the year. Allen and Unwin had high hopes for the book but was unprepared for its success. By Christmas of 1937, the first printing of *The Hobbit* was sold out. Realizing that he had a new, best-selling children's author in his hands, Stanley Unwin asked Tolkien to begin work right away on a sequel.

6 *The Lord of the Rings*

After a lifetime of creating languages, poems, and stories, J.R.R. Tolkien enjoyed his first commercial success at the age of forty-five. His publisher clamored for another book to ride on the success of the *The Hobbit*. He sent them a number of the other stories he had written for his children over the years, including "Roverandom," "Mr. Bliss," and "Farmer Giles of Ham," but all were rejected. What people really wanted, Allen and Unwin said, was more hobbits.

How About an Epic?

Tolkien did not have any other hobbit stories, but he did have *The Silmarillion*. At the time, there was no real connection between the two works. However, *The Silmarillion* was set in a similar ancient world populated by elves and dragons. At last, Tolkien reasoned, this might be the right time to publish his life's work.

He packed up his stacks of disorganized manuscripts and sent them off to Allen and Unwin. Much to his dismay, *The Silmarillion* was immediately rejected. The publisher had wanted another children's story, not a complex work featuring long lists of characters and difficult names. Tolkien un-

derstood but felt wounded by the rejection.

Though Allen and Unwin felt *The Silmarillion* was not a suitable followup to *The Hobbit*, the publisher did think it had potential value. One story in the collection drew particular praise—the one closest to Tolkien's heart; "Of Beren and Luthien." Stanley Unwin suggested that Tolkien look at *The Silmarillion* as "a rich mine to be explored in writing further books like *The Hobbit*."[46]

The New Hobbit

With the encouragement of his publisher, Tolkien set to work right away on a sequel. The work was unnamed for quite some time, simply referred to as "The New Hobbit." By December 1937, just months after *The Hobbit*'s publication, he had submitted the first chapter. Though progress on the first section of the book was rapid, it would take twelve years to finish the story and another five to publish it. The project became a primary focus of his life.

The book he began writing in 1937 was very different from the finished product. Originally it was another children's story whose central character was Bilbo Baggins's son, Bingo. According to the original premise, Bingo had spent his father's riches and set out in search of more. Over time, Bingo's character became a nephew, Frodo, and later still a casual note scribbled in the margin of the first draft revealed what would become the true focus of the story: "Make *return of ring* a motive."[47]

Tolkien had been wondering about the origin of the ring Bilbo acquired in *The Hobbit*. In devising the ring's history, Tolkien began to incorporate elements of his old tales from his beloved *Silmarillion* and soon realized that his furry-footed hobbits were the ideal vehicle for sharing his mythology with England and the world. The *Silmarillion* was a heroic epic that seemed to appeal only to scholars and linguists. The general public wanted easier-to-read entertainment. So he decided that he would dress up some of his old ideas in a new format. His publisher and audience seemed able to relate to an otherworldly realm of epic heroes, monsters, and magic as long as it was seen through the eyes of a simple country hobbit.

From this point, the plot took off virtually on its own. Though he consciously decided to base the tale, now called *The Lord of the Rings*, on the history and events of his Middle Earth, he found that the story was going in new, unexpected directions. The only thing he claimed to have known from the early stages was that Frodo was on a mission to reach the heart of the enemy's territory, the only place where the immeasurable evil of the One Ring could

"THE NEW HOBBIT"

In struggling to produce a sequel to The Hobbit, *Tolkien's "New Hobbit" became a more adult tale, taking on darker themes and building upon the rich mythology he had created for Middle Earth in* The Silmarillion.

In *The Hobbit*, Bilbo finds a magic ring with the power to make him invisible. The concept of rings of power was prevalent in many of the Norse mythologies Tolkien drew from, central also to the *Elder Edda* and Wagner's operatic *Ring* cycle. Eventually, he began to realize that the story of "The New Hobbit" was fertile ground in which to reawaken the extensive mythology of Middle Earth he had created over so many years. A full year after he had begun his sequel, he decided that Bilbo's ring was not just *a* ring of power, but *the* ring of power, the One Ring created by the dark lord Sauron to rule all the other rings and hence all the races of men, elves, and dwarves in Middle Earth. It was at this point that the book finally found the name by which it would be published many years later, *The Lord of the Rings*.

"On Fairy–Stories"

The following is from the introduction to a lecture Tolkien delivered in 1938 at St. Andrew's University, titled "On Fairy-Stories." The lecture explained the professor's philosophy of the nature of fantasy literature and remains one of the most well known treatises on the genre.

"I propose to speak about fairy-stories, though I am aware that this is a rash adventure. Faerie is a perilous land, and in it are pitfalls for the unwary and dungeons for the overbold. And overbold I may be accounted, for though I have been a lover of fairy-stories since I learned to read, and have at times thought about them, I have not studied them professionally. I have been hardly more than a wandering explorer (or trespasser) in the land, full of wonder but not of information.

The realm of fairy-story is wide and deep and high and filled with many things: all manner of beasts and birds are found there; shoreless seas and stars uncounted; beauty that is an enchantment, and an ever-present peril; both joy and sorrow as sharp as swords. In that realm a man may, perhaps, count himself fortunate to have wandered, but its very richness and strangeness tie the tongue of a traveler who would report them. And while he is there it is dangerous for him to ask too many questions, lest the gates should be shut and the keys be lost."

The importance of fairies and fairy stories was the subject of a 1938 lecture Tolkien gave at St. Andrew's University.

be destroyed forever. Everything else that happens seems to have surprised Tolkien as much as it would enthrall his future readers.

The Story Unfolds

As always, Tolkien felt that he was not in control of his story's direction. Tolkien's old notion about recording glimpses of a true history, rather than inventing a fiction of his own, reached a new level. *The Lord of the Rings* unfolded in rapid bursts at first. New characters would "appear" and he would have to figure out who they were and what kind of role they would play in the story. New plot twists completely changed the direction he assumed the story was taking. As Tolkien put it, "All the things I tried to write ahead of time just to direct myself proved to be no good when I got there. The story was written backwards as well as forward."[48]

At some point he found the book had fundamentally changed. When the terrifying Black Riders arrived in the story to hunt Frodo down, Tolkien realized that this was no longer a children's tale. The riders were undead spirits that had become slaves to an evil will, pursuing the Ring wherever it went. Tolkien wrote to his publisher, who had been waiting for quite some time already for his "new hobbit," to say that "stories tend to get out of hand, and this has taken an unprecedented turn."[49] He spent a long time mulling over the question of where this book would fit into the market. The *Silmarillion* was clearly for adults and *The Hobbit* for children; who would be the target audience for *The Lord of the Rings*?

On Fairy Stories

Tolkien's questions about the nature of fantasy stories and their proper audience led him to deliver one of the most memorable lectures of his life. While his lecture on *Beowulf* was the defining moment of his academic career, "On Fairy–Stories" was to become the defining moment of not only his commercial career but perhaps the genre of fantasy literature.

The occasion was the honorary Andrew Lang lecture at St. Andrew's University in Scotland in March 1939. Tolkien began by pointing out the important role that fantasy literature can play in the lives of both children and adults. He went on to discuss the elements that make up a successful fantasy story. These essentials, such as a clear relationship between the mundane primary world and the fantastic secondary world, and eliciting the reader's willing suspension of disbelief, became the blueprint of the genre. Tolkien did not invent these concepts, but he presented them in such clear and well-defined terms that the lecture lived on as a widely published essay, and today many writers of fantasy follow these basic guidelines when creating their own surreal worlds.

He explained that when an author succeeds, readers view the story not as a fiction, but as a real place that exists somewhere just outside their ability to see. One reviewer for the *New Statesman and Nation* confirmed Tolkien's own ability to do this when he described *The Hobbit* as giving its readers "the impression of a well-informed glimpse into the life of a wide other-world; a world wholly real, and with a quite matter-of-fact, supernatural natural history of its own."[50]

One of the threads Tolkien weaves through the essay is his concept of "sub-creation." Tolkien believed as a Christian that humans were made in the image of God, and that their noblest pursuit was thus to emulate God's greatest work: creation. To Tolkien, creation itself was strictly the domain of God, but he felt that all people had this power of sub-creation that, when tapped, brought them closest to God. He pointed out that people do so, on some level, all the time through creative expression such as art or music. As a fantasy author, he felt that through divine inspiration, he was able to sub-create entire worlds.

A VERY SLOW PROCESS

Sub-creation, in Tolkien's case, was not to be hurried. In December 1942, five years after he had begun, Tolkien wrote to his publisher that he had completed thirty-one chapters of *The Lord of the Rings* and he thought he would need only six more to finish. By the time he was done—seven years later—his final six chapters had grown into another thirty-one.

Many factors contributed to the long delays. As usual, the primary cause was his obsessive perfectionism. He took the notion of sub-creation so seriously that he would not tolerate any inconsistencies or illogic in the functioning of his world. His

son Christopher drew an elaborate map of the terrain to help him figure out where his characters were going and how long it should realistically take them to get there. Today the creation and inclusion of a highly detailed map of the fantasy world is a common artifice in fantasy literature, but the device was virtually unheard-of before Tolkien. The map made possible precise (and time-consuming) calculations of time, distance, the direction of the wind, and even the phases of the moon.

The responsibilities and stresses of his daily life were also getting in the way of his work on the book. He had been promoted from professor of Anglo-Saxon to the distinguished post of Merton Professor of English Language and Literature at Oxford, with all of its professional demands. He continued to meet regularly with the Inklings, with whom he shared the latest installments of the *The Lord of the Rings*. Edith was ill and he spent a lot of time tending to her. Also, Tolkien was writing amid the severe strain of World War II. As the war progressed, life in England came to a virtual standstill. Rations on everything from food to writing paper took his focus off his work, as did worry about his sons Michael and John, who were fighting in Europe. (Both survived the war.)

AN END IN SIGHT

After several years of slow progress on the book, Tolkien ran into an old friend. Rayner Unwin, who at age ten had written the first review of *The Hobbit,* was now an undergraduate at Oxford. In the summer

J.R.R. Tolkien took many years to complete The Lord of the Rings. *Meticulous attention to detail, personal strain, and the onset of World War II delayed its completion.*

of 1947, Tolkien decided to show a nearly complete version of *The Lord of the Rings* to him. Rayner reported to his father—Tolkien's publisher—that the tale was a bit strange but brilliant. Tolkien was encouraged by this assessment.

However, another delay occurred when he realized that some details of *The Hobbit* had to be changed in order to be consistent with the story that had evolved as its "sequel." He produced a revised edition of *The Hobbit* that was published in late 1947. After two more years of exhaustive scrutiny of *The Lord of the Rings*, he at last had a typed and complete first draft. In 1949 he sent it to Stanley Unwin with a note stating, "It is written in my life-blood, such as that is, thick or thin; and I can no other."[51]

PUBLISHING WARS

Another five years would pass, however, before it reached publication, in large part

---

LEAF BY NIGGLE

At the age of fifty-one, Tolkien became obsessed with worry that he might never finish The Lord of the Rings, *on which he had labored for years. The very thought of it often sent him into a dark mood and kept him from getting any work done at all. After a long bout of dealing with this fear and the depression that was borne of it, he found a way to exorcise his demons through a different short story.*

He woke up one day with a tale in his head and felt compelled to put it down on paper. The story concerned a man named Niggle, but it may as well have been about Tolkien himself. Niggle was an artist who spent all his free time painting in the shed in his backyard. His most treasured painting was that of a large tree. The act of painting it brought him great joy, but he could never finish it, as he spent so much time "niggling" over the details of every line and shadow on leaf.

Niggle constantly worried that the distractions in his daily life were keeping him from completing his work. Eventually, he died (in a sense) without finishing it, but found his beloved tree in the next world. What he had so lovingly "sub-created" in life had become real in this other world. His tree was no longer a painting, but a real tree, complete with the beautiful landscape he had painted around it.

The story, "Leaf by Niggle," was eventually published together with his lecture "On Fairy Stories" as the book *Tree and Leaf.* The story, combined with pressure from C.S. Lewis to get on with his work, helped him to move past his fears and continue work on *The Lord of the Rings.*

---

because of haggling over one very important detail: *The Silmarillion.* Allen and Unwin had made it clear that it was only interested in *The Lord of the Rings* and not his epic mythology of Middle Earth. Tolkien wanted a package deal.

One of the Inklings introduced Tolkien to a friend who worked for Collins, a competing publishing house also interested in *The Lord of the Rings.* When Collins agreed to publish both books, he offered *The Lord of the Rings* to Collins. Unsure of his obligation to Allen and Unwin, he wrote to his editors there, trying to make *The Lord of the Rings* sound as unappealing as possible. He described the manuscript as a long, complex, and bitter tale, unfit for children. When they still showed interest in the book, he followed up with an ultimatum that Allen and Unwin must take either both books or nothing. The publisher declined both.

He was now free to work with Collins, but eventually he would regret this decision. Collins claimed that at nearly a thousand pages *The Lord of the Rings* was far too long and needed serious cutting. Tolkien the perfectionist had spent many years revising and refining his manuscript and felt virtually every word was essential to the story and the world he had created. He could not bear significant alterations. After two and a half years of contract negotiations, he broke off relations with Collins and took *The Lord of the Rings* back to Allen and Unwin. He wrote to his old friend Rayner, who was now working at the firm with his father, "Years are becoming precious. What about *The Lord of the Rings*? Can

anything be done . . . to unlock gates I slammed myself?"[52]

THE RING FINDS A HOME

Rayner Unwin, who had always wanted to publish the story, seized his chance. He wrote to his father, who was out of the country, describing *The Lord of the Rings* as a work of genius, that probably would not make a lot of money. With the skyrocketing cost of paper, the lengthy book would be very expensive to produce. Combined with the lack of a clear market for the book, it presented a big risk, one he estimated could lose about a thousand pounds, a substantial sum in 1952. The senior Unwin replied, "If you think it a work of genius, then you may lose £1,000."[53]

Rayner contacted Tolkien with the news that Allen and Unwin would publish *The Lord of the Rings* without major alterations. He set two conditions, though. First, to reduce printing costs, the book would be divided into three parts and released in three installments over a period of a year. For this reason many people refer to the book as a trilogy, though it was written as one continuous story. The second condition was an unusual royalty agreement. Instead of paying Tolkien a fixed sum as an advance and then a small percentage of net sales profit as was typical, Rayner offered Tolkien no advance but a commitment to pay the author a whopping 50 percent of future profits if the publisher recouped its initial costs. In short, Allen and Unwin was trying to cut back on inital costs in case the book did not sell.

Tolkien desperately wanted to publish his book, so he agreed to Rayner's terms. In the end, this arrangement proved enormously profitable to the aging professor.

AT LONG LAST

After another eighteen months of production meetings and final revisions the first installment of *The Lord of the Rings,* titled *The Fellowship of the Ring,* was released in the summer of 1954. Tolkien, who was extremely nervous about the reaction of critics, wrote to a friend, Father Robert Murray, "I am dreading the publication, for it will be impossible not to mind what is said. I have exposed my heart to be shot at."[54] Two days after the book arrived in bookstores, a review in *Time and Tide* declared,

> This book is like lightening from a clear sky. To say that in it heroic romance, gorgeous, eloquent, and unashamed, has suddenly returned at a period almost pathological in its anti-romanticism, is inadequate. . . . But in the history of Romance itself—a history which stretches back to the *Odyssey* and beyond—it makes not a return but an advance or revolution: the conquest of new territory.[55]

It must be said that this glowing review came from Tolkien's colleague and supporter C.S. Lewis. The rest of the reviews were decidedly mixed, setting the stage for the critical debate associated with Tolkien's work that continues to this day. Negative reviews ranged from complaints that the characters were simplistic in their portrayal of good or evil, to criticism of a lack of strong female characters, to mockery of the archaic writing style. Influential critic Edmund Wilson wrote in the *Nation* that Tolkien lacked creativity: "An impotence of imagination seems to me to sap the whole story."[56]

Negative reviews were offset by a number of positive critiques. The *Boston Herald Traveler* referred to it as "one of the best wonder-tales ever written."[57] A review in the *New Republic* ended by stating that it was one of the "very few works of genius in recent literature."[58] The debate, revolving around whether the book was a work of great literature or an overinflated fairy tale, was polarizing. One reviewer in the *New York Times* wrote, "Nobody seems to have a moderate opinion; either, like myself, people find it a masterpiece of the genre, or they cannot abide it."[59] While critics either loved it or hated it, the public response was more mild. The book did not fly off the shelves, but it sold at a very respectable rate. A U.S. edition was published a few months later by Houghton Mifflin, and also enjoyed steady sales.

In November 1954 the second installment, *The Two Towers,* was released. Sales climbed and people eagerly awaited the third installment. Fans began writing to the publisher demanding to know when it would come out and protesting the "protracted and intolerable suspense."[60] However, another year passed before *The Return of the King* was released.

Tolkien, again, was the cause of the delay. He was trying to complete an appendix to appear at the end of the third book, containing detailed time lines, family trees, calendars, and pronunciation guides. He

HARSH CRITICS

Literary critics were firmly split in their opinions of The Lord of the Rings. *Most had very strong feelings, either loving or hating it. Edmund Wilson's negative review, which appeared on April 14, 1956, in the* Nation, *was a rallying point among Tolkien detractors.*

"[*The Lord of the Rings*] is essentially a children's book, which has somehow gotten out of hand. . . . The author has indulged himself in developing the fantasy for its own sake. . . . Prose and verse are on the same level of professional amateurishness. . . . What we get is a simple confrontation—in more or less the traditional terms of British melodrama—of the forces of Evil with the forces of Good, the remote and alien villain with the plucky little home-grown hero. . . . Dr. Tolkien has little skill at narrative and no instinct for literary form. The characters talk a story-book language . . . and as personalities they do not impose themselves. At the end of this long romance, I still had no conception of the wizard Gandalf, who is a cardinal figure, and had never been able to visualize him at all. For the most part such characterizations as Dr. Tolkien is able to contrive are perfectly stereotyped: Frodo the good little Englishman. Samwise, his doglike servant, who talks lower-class and respectful, and never deserts his master. These characters who are no characters are involved in interminable adventures the poverty of invention displayed in which is, it seems to me, almost pathetic. . . . An impotence of imagination seems to me to sap the whole story."

Literary critic Edmund Wilson gave The Lord of the Rings *a scathing review.*

also intended to include an enormous amount of background material that he felt was important to the tale but had been pulled from the main body of the text for slowing the pace. In the end, under pressure from both his growing fan base and his publisher, he wrote a note of apology to the readers in the third volume and released it with the appendices only partially complete.

The work of nearly twenty years of Tolkien's life was now complete. Less than eighteen months after the first book was released, he received his first royalty payment from Allen and Unwin. It was thirty-five hundred pounds, more than his annual salary at Oxford. Sales continued to climb slowly but steadily, and over the next ten years he received larger and larger checks. He was overjoyed to be free of financial worry for the first time in his life. *The Lord of the Rings* was more successful than anyone had anticipated—but it was only the beginning.

7 The Later Years

In the 1960s critical debate over *The Lord of the Rings* continued to rage as sales of the book continued to climb. Tolkien, however, began to slow down. Now in his seventies, he grew more eccentric and more private, setting egg timers when journalists began their interviews and then promptly kicking them out when the bell rang. His attitude toward the modern world darkened with each year, and he bitterly objected as the English countryside he loved gave way to new cities, roads, and development. It pained him greatly, in particular, to see trees torn down; on one occasion, he referred to the chainsaw as "one of the greatest horrors of our age."[61] Increasingly intolerant of people's actions and words, he began strictly limiting the visitors he would allow into his home and spent most of his time with Edith and his grandchildren.

THE LOSS OF A FRIEND

In 1954 Tolkien's colleague C.S. Lewis had accepted a teaching position at Cambridge University. He commuted between Oxford and Cambridge, but the Inklings ceased to meet on a regular basis. This was a difficult adjustment for Tolkien, but made easier by the fact that their friendship had begun to cool in the last few years.

One reason for this may have been simple competition. Lewis was a far more prolific writer than Tolkien and the old professor may have envied the other man's ability to produce book after book. Tolkien became increasingly critical of Lewis's work in later years. He was very open about his dislike of Lewis's *Narnia* books, thinking their style was too simple and condescending to children. He also never forgave Lewis for not becoming a Catholic when he embraced Christianity.

The final blow apparently came when Lewis married very late in life and no longer found much time for his old friends. Tolkien felt that the lifelong bachelor had been unfairly demanding of his own time earlier in life, never accepting or understanding Tolkien's family obligations. Now that Lewis had these same obligations, he was rarely seen by his friends. Despite this estrangement, the pair kept in touch, and Tolkien was severely shaken by Lewis's death in 1963; he wrote to his daughter Priscilla that it felt "like an axe-blow near the roots."[62]

In 1959 Tolkien, shown here with wife Edith, retired from teaching at Oxford University.

RETIREMENT

In 1959, at the age of sixty-seven, Tolkien retired from his professorship at Oxford. That year he delivered the commencement speech to the graduating class, in which he shared his fondness for the institution but chastised it for changing many of its grand traditions. He ended the speech with an Elven poem from *The Fellowship of the Ring* called "Namarie," sung in farewell by Galadriel, queen of the elves, to Frodo and his companions as they leave her enchanted realm.

Financially secure, at last he had the freedom and time to work on his long list of shelved projects. He worked at a Modern English translation of *Sir Gawain and the Green Knight* and a poem called "Pearl," which was thought to be the only other work by the same Middle English author. Now that Tolkien was a well-known author, publishers sought rights to publish his earlier work, so he began editing many of his old stories for publication. However, the work he valued most, *The Silmarillion*, continued to languish. After sixty years, the stories were still in a complete state of disarray, despite Tolkien's continued attempts to assimilate them into a publishable form.

THE WAR OVER MIDDLE EARTH

By the early 1960s, the popularity of *The Lord of the Rings* seemed to be waning. In 1961 a reviewer for the London *Observer*, who was not a fan of the book, wrote that Tolkien's work seemed to have, at last,

"passed into merciful oblivion."[63] This assessment turned out to be false. Just a few years later, a bizarre publishing dispute turned what had once been merely a moderately successful book into a phenomenon, unprecedented in the realm of fantasy literature.

Until 1965, *The Lord of the Rings* had been available only in a hardcover edition. At that time an American publishing house, Ace Books, decided to take advantage of loose copyright laws and publish its own unauthorized paperback version. Ace did not seek Tolkien's permission or offer him any royalties. Allen and Unwin immediately asked the professor to make some quick revisions to the story, which it intended to reissue in the United States under strict copyright and prevent Ace from publishing its version.

Tolkien agreed but was characteristically slow. By the time he was finished, Ace's mass market paperback was already in print. Ace was firmly established in the science fiction and fantasy market and its low-priced paperback edition attracted a whole new, younger audience. The book began to sell by the thousands.

Several months later, the authorized U.S. paperback edition of *The Lord of the Rings* was published by Ballantine Books. It contained a note from Tolkien explaining that this was the only authorized version of his book and asking people who "approve of courtesy to living authors"[64] to purchase no other. Ballantine, of course, had to pay royalties to the author, and its edition cost twenty cents more than the Ace paperback; most people were unmoved by the copyright issue and continued to buy the unauthorized book.

At this point, Tolkien took matters into his own hands. For the previous ten years, his failure to meet deadlines on other projects often had been blamed on his nearly obsessive desire to answer his fan mail. He had responded to countless letters and developed an on-going correspondence with dozens of fans and members of various literary and publishing circles. He began to use this network of contacts to build a movement against Ace Books, including in every piece of mail a letter explaining the situation and asking for people to voice their opinions and support him against what he considered moral piracy. Sales of the Ballantine version began to pick up and eventually, through pressure from the public as well as the Science Fiction Writers of America, Ace agreed to stop printing Tolkien's books and pay him back royalties. Tolkien had won what one journalist referred to as "the war over Middle Earth."[65]

THE SPOILS OF WAR

The publishing battle over Tolkien's Middle Earth had garnered tremendous media attention that amounted to free advertising. Sales of the affordable paperbacks boomed. One hundred thousand copies of the Ace edition were sold during the year it was on the market; six months later, the Ballantine edition passed the 1 million mark.

The phenomenon continued in America and around the world. *The Lord of the Rings* became enormously popular among teenagers and college students, who made it an icon of the sixties counterculture. Young people of that era, increasingly dissatisfied with materialistic values, began seeking other nontraditional guideposts in life, such as spiritualism, Eastern philosophies, the occult, psychedelic drugs, and a return to a simpler way of life. Tolkien's messages about romantic values, preserving the natural world, and rebelling against industrialization struck a powerful chord on American college campuses in the 1960s.

Tolkien Societies sprang up all over the world, from Harvard and London to such remote locales as Vietnam and the island of Borneo. In the United States, lapel badges bearing slogans such as "Frodo Lives" or "Gandalf for President" became the hot trend on college campuses. Graffiti appeared on the walls of New York and London subways bearing messages such as "J.R.R. Tolkien Is Hobbit-Forming."[66] Colleges renamed campus roads after Tolkien or his characters, whose names entered popular culture, for example, in the magazine title *Gandalf's Garden*—a psychedelic mixture of gardening tips and new age articles. By 1968 *The Lord of the Rings* had been translated into eighteen languages and had sold nearly 10 million copies, making it one of the best-selling works of fiction to date.

THE PROFESSOR IN THE SPOTLIGHT

Overnight, the quiet and increasingly reclusive retired professor became a pop culture icon. His fan mail arrived by the truckload and Allen and Unwin had to provide him with a part-time secretary, Joy Hill, to help answer the mail and keep his affairs in order. At first, he was amused and a little bewildered by all the attention, but he took great care to answer as many letters as he could.

He routinely received invitations to attend meetings of various Tolkien Societies and on one occasion, he accepted. A bookseller in Holland wanted to host a Hobbit feast in his honor. People arrived in droves, dressed as characters from the book. Tolkien devotees read poems and performed songs in Elvish, and the delighted author himself provided the grand finale. Tolkien delivered a rousing speech in a mixture of English, Dutch, and Elvish which warned against the impending onslaught of industrialization in the world.

THE SPOTLIGHT HEATS UP

Tolkien, while concerned about the fanaticism attached to his book, was nonetheless

---

A PLEA TO HIS FANS

In 1965 an unauthorized paperback edition of The Lord of the Rings *was released and became a best-seller in the United States. Several months later, the authorized edition was released with the following note from Tolkien imploring readers to purchase this and no other version.*

"I hope that those who have read *The Lord of the Rings* with pleasure will not think me ungrateful: to please readers was my main object, and to be assured of this has been a great reward. Nonetheless, for all its defects of omission and inclusion, it was the product of long labor, and like a simple-minded hobbit I feel that it is, while I am still alive, my property in justice unaffected by copyright laws. It seems to me a grave discourtesy, to say no more, to issue my book without even a polite note informing me of the project: dealings one might expect of Saruman in his decay rather than from the defenders of the West. However that may be, this paperback edition and no other has been published with my consent and cooperation. Those who approve of courtesy (at least) to living authors will purchase it and no other. And if the many kind readers who have encouraged me with their letters will add to their courtesy by referring friends or enquirers to Ballantine Books, I shall be very grateful. To them, and to all who have been pleased by this book, especially those Across the Water for whom it is specially intended, I dedicate this volume."

THE TOLKIEN SOCIETY OF AMERICA

As the attention of readers around the world was drawn to The Lord of the Rings *in the mid-1960s, a variety of Tolkien clubs sprang up across the globe. In* J.R.R. Tolkien: Architect of Middle Earth, *Daniel Grotta describes the way in which the Tolkien Society of America came into being in New York City.*

"In February, 1965, the first formal Tolkien Society came about through the odd medium of subway graffiti. A brilliant fifteen-year-old high school student named Richard Plotz had been attending Saturday morning science classes at Columbia University and happened to see 'something written in Elvish on a poster in the station. It had to be Elvish, but I didn't believe it. Who could write things in Elvish? The next week the writing was gone, but someone had written BILBO BAGGINS IS PROBABLY A FAKE on another poster.' The running dialogue between unknown Tolkien addicts continued for some weeks until Plotz impulsively scribbled TOLKIEN CLUB MEETS AT ALMA MATER STATUE [on the Columbia campus], 2:00, FEBRUARY FIFTH. A week later, six students—none of whom knew one another—braved the twenty degree weather and met beneath the statue for an hour. Incidentally, 'the subway writing still continued; none of those people had been writing it! I realized that Tolkien was a force to be reckoned with, so I put an ad in the *New Republic* that said 'Discuss hobbit lore and learn Elvish,' and signed it Frodo, with my address. My first reply was from a man in Norman, Oklahoma, who was doing his doctoral thesis on the names in Tolkien's books; I got about seventy letters.'"

Since 1965 fans like this man have gathered at the author's Society of America functions to discuss Tolkien's works.

heartened by the way his messages appeared to speak to people of all cultures. He commented:

> Many young Americans are involved in the stories in a way that I am not. But they do use this sometimes as a means against some abomination. There was one campus . . . where the council of the university pulled down a very pleasant little grove of trees to make way for what they called a 'culture center' out of some sort of concrete blocks. The students were outraged. They wrote ANOTHER BIT OF MORDOR on it.[67]

His popularity seemed to have no bounds. In 1968 the BBC produced a documentary about the professor called *Tolkien in Oxford*. He enjoyed some of this attention, but soon it began to overwhelm him. People were sending him gifts of every kind including paintings, tobacco, food, wine, art, and even photographs of themselves dressed as characters from *The Lord of the Rings*. His address and phone number were listed in the Oxford telephone directory so not surprisingly he began to get calls and visitors to his home. Strangers would show up on his doorstep, looking for autographs, or pictures, or just to meet him. Overseas calls would come at all hours of the night. Even the flower garden outside his window was destroyed by people climbing through it in hopes of getting a snapshot of the professor in his sitting room.

ONE LAST STORY

Though he was now famous and wealthy beyond his wildest imaginings, the dark moods that used to overtake him from time to time became more pronounced and more frequent in his old age. One of these bouts of depression resulted in the story "Smith of Wooton Major." He was actually attempting to write an introduction for a new edition of one of his favorite childhood fantasy books, George MacDonald's *The Golden Key*. In discussing the meaning of the term *fairy* he began to give an example of a typical fairy story. As was often the case, this story took on a life of its own and the introduction was never finished. "Smith of Wooton Major" was about a young man given the opportunity to walk through a fantastic world, knowing that it would soon be over and he would have to return to the drab reality of the real world. It reflected Tolkien's current lackluster attitude toward the world in his old age, and his fears of growing old. Released in 1967, it would be the last story that Tolkien wrote.

AN EXIT FROM OXFORD

Tolkien had always loved his wife, Edith, but they grew even closer in his retirement. In 1966 they celebrated their fiftieth wedding anniversary at an elaborate party, held at Merton College. Among the highlights was a surprise guest, a composer named Donald Swann, who had set one of Tolkien's Elvish poems to music. His performance of "The Road Goes Ever On" touched the professor deeply.

At the age of seventy-nine, Edith's health was failing and Tolkien became increasingly concerned about her. She had always seemed happiest when they spent time with her friends in the seaside vacation/retirement community of Bournemouth. Though he still loved the university and would miss his friends, the constant barrage of fans and journalists had made life there unbearable for the two of them. So in 1968 they packed up their belongings, sold their house, and for the first time in forty-three years, moved from Oxford.

BOURNEMOUTH

Edith was happier than she had ever been in their new seaside retirement community. For the first time in her life, she had a large circle of friends and enjoyed spending time socializing with them. Though Tolkien felt cut off from his old friends and children, seeing Edith so happy was satisfaction enough. He also enjoyed the freedom from his fans. From his new, unlisted address, he could continue correspondences at his leisure and at his discretion. Joy Hill made weekly trips to Bournemouth to assist him and they became close friends in his later years.

He continued to work on *The Silmarillion*, but found himself sidetracked by the technical details of designing worlds. He wrote elaborate essays, for example, on the relationship between the aging processes of men and elves and on the nature of plants and animals in Middle Earth. Ironing out the intimate details, which helped to bring more realism to his sub-created world, brought him great joy and often superceded the need to finish his work. After three years of living in Bournemouth, he had

made some progress on his work. However, in November of 1971, Edith died at age eighty-two and his life changed again.

BACK TO OXFORD

Though Edith had been in failing health, Tolkien was still shaken by her death. He could barely imagine life without the woman he had been married to for fifty-five years. His only other friends and family were back in Oxford, so he decided to return there to live out the remainder of his days.

His old college, Merton, put him up in an apartment, provided him with caretakers who lived downstairs, and welcomed him to take all his meals in the faculty dining halls. He thoroughly enjoyed being back at Oxford and became friendly with the married couple who looked after him. He spent time with their children as well as his own grandchildren and was surprisingly active at age eighty.

He took every opportunity to socialize with his old friends and colleagues. Joy Hill would spend hours walking through the Oxford Botanical Gardens with Tolkien, until she could no longer keep up. He also spent a lot of time entertaining every kind of merchandising offer imaginable concerning his books. Most of these he turned down, as he was always fearful that someone else's interpretation of his work would not agree with his own.

In June 1972, Oxford conferred upon him an honorary doctorate. This would be the fourth of five such degrees awarded to him, and the most meaningful. The university was quick to point out that the de-

FULL-TIME FAN MAIL

As he grew older, Tolkien could not keep up with the enormous bulk of fan mail he received. His publishers provided him with a part-time secretary, Joy Hill, who grew close to the old professor during his final years. In an interview for the London Times, *she describes the vast multitude of mail he received.*

"They came from all over the world, they came in English, French, Spanish, German, Italian and Elvish, they came in conventional and psychedelic envelopes, they came in packets and with gifts, they arrived three times a day six days a week, they have been arriving for years and they are still coming; the trickle has become a stream, a river, a flood. . . . They send questions galore, even parcels of them, some 'to be opened only when the author has completed his next book.' 'Why did you kill . . . ?' 'What was the reason for . . . ?' 'Is there a connection . . . ?' 'What happened to . . . ?' 'I am asking you with tears in my eyes to take me on as a student.' 'Please call me first thing in the morning your time on the 21st.' 'I am crazy about you.' 'I am reading your beautiful story and still weeping.' 'The prose can only be compared to the King James Bible.' 'Admit Middle-earth to the U.N.'"

gree was conferred for his academic accomplishments and not his commercial success. Also in 1972 he traveled to Buckingham Palace in London, where he was made a Commander of the Order of the British Empire by Queen Elizabeth. The CBE, as the title is known, is one step below knighthood, an honor people theorized Tolkien would have received as well. In the summer of 1973, however, he contracted pneumonia and died on September 2 at age eighty-one.

PUBLISHING A MYTH

Fans and friends mourned Tolkien's death. Memorials were held all over the world, celebrating a man who lived most of his life in obscurity, but died a hero to millions. A tribute in the *Guardian* summarized his significance:

> [Tolkien] stands as a unique figure in literature. While drawing inspiration from the style and mode of Celtic, Norse, and Teutonic folklore, based on a lifetime's professional practice of textual criticism, he revived for himself, after a thousand years' lapse, the role of the epic minstrel; took up again, to popular acclaim in the twentieth century, the immemorial theme of the Quest: the heroic attempt of puny mortals to resolve the agelong cosmic conflict of good and evil.[68]

For the Love of Luthien

Upon his wife's death, Tolkien began sharing many of his thoughts and feelings with his children. Carpenter's The Letters of J.R.R. Tolkien *contains a letter he wrote to his son Christopher explaining the deep love he had for Edith and why he wanted to put a name from one of his favorite stories on her tombstone.*

"I have at last gotten busy about Mummy's grave.... The inscription I should like is:

EDITH MARY TOLKIEN
1889-1971
Luthien

brief and [simple], except for *Luthien*, which says for me more than a multitude of words: for she was (and knew she was) my Luthien.

... I will say no more now. But I should like ere long to have a long talk with *you*. For if as seems probable I shall never write any ordered biography—it is against my nature, which expresses itself about things deepest felt in tales and myths—someone close in heart to me should know something about things that records do not record: the dreadful sufferings of our childhoods, from which we rescued one another, but could not wholly heal the wounds that later often proved disabling; the sufferings that we endured after our love began—all of which (over and above our personal weaknesses) might help to make pardonable, or understandable, the lapses and darknesses which at times marred our lives—and to explain how these never touched our depths nor dimmed our memories of our youthful love. For ever (especially when alone) we still met in the woodland glade, and went hand in hand many times to escape the shadow of imminent death before our last parting."

Tolkien etched a name from one of his favorite stories on Edith's tombstone as a tribute to his wife.

While he had accomplished much in his life, he had left *The Silmarillion* unfinished. Realizing in his old age that this might be the case, he worked extensively in his final years with the only person who was nearly as familiar with the mythology as he was, his son Christopher. By this time a professor of language at Oxford himself, Christopher Tolkien took on the task of completing his father's work and sharing it with the world. At the age of fifty, Christopher retired from teaching to devote himself to the project full-time. In 1977, sixty years after it was begun, *The Silmarillion* at last was introduced to the world. Although it was marketed as a novel, Christopher had tried to keep it what his father intended it to be: an authentic epic, best appreciated when read aloud. *The Silmarillion* was met with mixed reviews. One reviewer for the *Washington Post* called it "a creation of singular beauty."[69] Other critics, however, did not appreciate the endless torrent of names and still others complained that the archaic wording made reading too difficult.

Regardless of the critics, bookstores could not keep copies on the shelves. The initial printing in America ran to seven hundred thousand copies and still the publisher had to subcontract additional printing presses to meet demands. True Tolkien fans were thrilled by the work and over the years Christopher continued to release new volumes of his father's history of Middle Earth that could not fit into the original *Silmarillion*. Though Tolkien died more than thirty years ago, his legacy lives on. To this day, new books, music, poetry, art, and movies continue to spring up around the ageless mythology of J.R.R. Tolkien.

The Legacy

J.R.R. Tolkien's work has been the subject of thousands of popular and academic articles, books, and doctoral dissertations for more than forty years. Tolkien scholarship and criticism now makes up a substantial body of serious work, and his legions of fans have achieved cult status. The author, however, disliked much of this analysis and simply wanted readers to enjoy the story. He felt that *The Lord of the Rings* had become his *Beowulf*.

ALLEGORY

The literary analyses that Tolkien objected to most were interpretations of *The Lord of the Rings* as an allegory of World War II. Many people dissected similarities between the allies of the West—Gondor and Rohan—with real-world equivalents, the United States and Great Britain. The foes of the East—Sauron and Saruman—were said to represent the dictators Hitler and Mussolini. Tolkien adamantly denied that the story was allegorical in any sense. He pointed out that the story was meant as a

myth, in which a classic struggle between good and evil was being waged that could be applicable to any number of modern events. "I cordially dislike allegory," he once said, "in all its manifestations, and always have done so. . . . I think that many confuse applicability with allegory; but the one resides in the freedom of the reader, and the other in the purported domination of the author."[70]

RELIGIOUS SIGNIFICANCE

Tolkien was a staunch Catholic; not surprisingly, many papers and entire books have explored religious symbolism in *The Lord of the Rings.* Some claim that Gandalf, Aragorn, or even Frodo are representations of Christ. Other elements of the story have been described as symbols of God, the Virgin Mary, heaven, and hell. While Tolkien denied that the story was an allegory of Christianity, he did comment on more than one occasion that it incorporated Christian values. He also believed that his mythology was not incompatible with that of Western religion. It features one god, Eru; a system of angels, the Valar; and the mortal creatures made in the god's image, man. Middle Earth simply had an additional level of existence between the angels and humans—Elves, who were given the gift, and the curse, of immortality.

In a letter he wrote in 1958, Tolkien explained that if there was one primary theme in the book, it would be "Death and Immortality."[71] He explained that the pursuit of immortality was foolish, as it is only the finite nature of life that motivates mortal men and women to accomplish their great works.

MORE THAN A BOOK

In the nearly fifty years since its original publication, *The Lord of the Rings* has evolved from one of the best-selling books in history into an empire, with connections to every entertainment market. It has inspired serial radio dramas, original music compositions, artwork, calendars, postcards, toys, video games, a comical parody called *Bored of the Rings,* and an animated film. It even spawned a new genre of entertainment when an American insurance salesman, Gary Gygax, was inspired by it to quit his job and create a game, Dungeons and Dragons, in which people assumed the personas of wizards or warriors and acted out their deeds in live-action role play.

People who consider Tolkien's popularity a fad have wondered when the fascination with his books would finally wear off. In 1999, one journalist speculated that "if technology makes the written word redundant, Tolkien's work may founder. His books, which have proved too real [too vivid and detailed] to be reproduced by any of the new forms of virtual reality, may then be forgotten."[72]

Instead, however, technology seems to have breathed new life into Tolkien's work. In 2001 the first installment of a new live-action feature film version of *The Lord of the Rings* was released. Created by a team of Tolkien purists led by director Peter Jackson, the film was years in the making. To preserve the continuity, as well as to reduce costs, it was filmed as a single production to be released in three installments at yearly intervals, much like the book itself. An article in *Time* magazine referred to the project as "the riskiest endeavor in motion-picture history,"[73] because of its $300 million price tag. Having already paid to produce all three movies, if the first one bombed, the producers risked huge financial losses.

Again in moviemaking, as in publishing, the gamble paid off. Tolkien fanatics and newcomers to the story alike turned out in droves and loved it. The first film, *The Fellowship of the Ring,* was nominated for thirteen Academy Awards, including best picture, and earned more than $860 million worldwide. The second installment, *The Two Towers,* earned over $917 million, making it the fifth-highest-grossing film in history, with *Fellowship* two notches behind at number seven.

A NEW MARKET

As an imaginative teenager in the T.C.B.S., Tolkien believed he was destined for great things. Perhaps Tolkien's most significant legacy is the way his work revealed the untapped commercial potential of fantasy literature. As a contemporary of his puts it, "[Tolkien opened] up a new continent of imaginative space for many millions of readers, and hundreds of writers—though he himself would have said that it was an old continent which he was merely rediscovering."[74]

Certainly fantasy literature long predates *The Lord of the Rings.* Tales of the fantastic stretch back as far as Homer's *Odyssey* and Milton's *Paradise Lost.* Even modern fantasy literature existed before Tolkien, such as Lewis Carroll's *Alice in Wonderland* and L. Frank Baum's *The Wizard of Oz.* These books became quite famous in their own right, but, much like *The Hobbit,* they were primarily aimed at children. The concept of modern fantasy for adults was unexplored before Tolkien. *The Lord of the Rings,* which possessed not only literary value but ultimately tremendous commercial potential, was al-

Fans of Lord of the Rings, *dressed as characters from the book, line up to see* The Fellowship of the Ring, *attesting to the great popularity of Tolkien's work.*

TOLKIEN'S TIMELESS LEGACY

Writer Joseph Pearce comments on the timelessness of Tolkien's Lord of the Rings *in his book* Tolkien: A Celebration.

"By placing his epic in Middle-earth he can deal with eternal [truths] without the distractions of fads, fashions and the flood of ephemera which clutters modern life. If he had set his story in England during the 1940s, he would no doubt have been commended for his 'realism' by contemporary critics, but his 'modern' work would appear dated today and possibly less relevant and real to subsequent generations. Tolkien's sub-created world is timeless, enabling him to ignore the peripheral in favour of the perennial problems of existence. For this reason, *The Lord of the Rings* is no more dated today than it was when it was first published. For the same reason it is safe to predict its continued popularity. If future generations stop reading Tolkien's classic it will not be because it has become irrelevant or dated. Rather, if they stop reading Tolkien it will be because they have stopped reading."

most turned down by publishers who could not fathom its target audience.

Ultimately, as an article in the *New York Times* points out, Tolkien's work "succeeded more completely than any previous writer in this genre."[75] In response to his success, publishers began paying more attention to fantasy authors and the market grew by leaps and bounds. Today it is one of the largest segments of the publishing industry. In fact, the highest-grossing fiction in the history of the written word belongs to the modern fantasy genre: J.K. Rowling's *Harry Potter* series. These books, like so many others, owe their success to the publishing doors that were opened for them by Tolkien many years ago.

Tolkien's work changed the way publishers conducted their business, and the way authors crafted their fantasy novels. Tolkien's structure in *The Lord of the Rings* has been emulated by countless fantasy writers. The most common blueprint in fantasy literature today is the creation of a secondary world, full of magic, strange beasts, and strange places, yet similar enough to the primary world of the reader to make it accessible. Painstaking attention to the details of these worlds—creating maps, races of creatures, histories of invented civilizations, and entire vocabularies and mythologies—has also become a standard practice. In fact, Tolkien's shadow looms so large that most writers of fantasy quest novels today cannot avoid comparisons with him and struggle to establish individual identities.

The goal of most fantasy literature is to create a world that is at least as real as the one in which the reader lives. Many Tolkien fans claim that the world he created seems somehow *more* real than theirs. A contemporary of Tolkien's attempted to explain this notion, and Tolkien's extraordinary popularity, by saying that his work has a feel that you just can't get anywhere else. It is similar to the way that some portrait painters are able to put into a portrait more of a man than a photograph can get. A photograph gets only something which existed for a second when the light was just so, whereas the portrait painter gives us something far more of the man as he is through many, many moments and years.[76]

Notes

Introduction: The Man Behind the Rings

1. Quoted in Tom Shippey, *J.R.R. Tolkien: Author of the Century*. New York: Houghton Mifflin, 2000, p. 6.

2. Quoted in Humphrey Carpenter, *J.R.R. Tolkien: A Biography*. New York: Houghton Mifflin, 2000, p. 131.

Chapter 1: A Country Boy

3. Quoted in Carpenter, *J.R.R. Tolkien*, p. 22.

4. Quoted in Susan Ang, *The Master of the Ring*. Cambridge, England: Icon, 2002, pp. 13–14.

5. Quoted in Joseph Pearce, *Tolkien: A Celebration*. San Francisco: Ignatius, 2001, p. 75.

6. Quoted in Daniel Grotta, *J.R.R. Tolkien: Architect of Middle Earth*. Philadelphia: Running, 1992, p. 154.

7. Quoted in Carpenter, *J.R.R. Tolkien*, p. 30.

8. Quoted in Humphrey Carpenter and Christopher Tolkien, eds., *The Letters of J.R.R. Tolkien*. New York: Houghton Mifflin, 2000, p. 340.

Chapter 2: Unlocking the Doors of Language

9. Quoted in Carpenter, *J.R.R. Tolkien*, p. 44.

10. Quoted in Carpenter, *J.R.R. Tolkien*, p. 137.

11. Quoted in Ang, *The Master of the Rings*, p. 23.

12. Quoted in Anne E. Neimark, *Myth Maker: J.R.R. Tolkien*. Orlando, FL: Harcourt, Brace, 1996, p. 31.

13. Quoted in Alida Becker, *The Tolkien Scrapbook*. Philadelphia: Running, 1978, p. 12.

14. Quoted in Grotta, *J.R.R. Tolkien*, p. 27.

15. Quoted in Carpenter and Tolkien, *The Letters of J.R.R. Tolkien*, p. 214.

16. Quoted in Neimark, *Myth Maker*, p. 37.

17. Quoted in Bradley J. Birzer, *J.R.R. Tolkien's Sanctifying Myth*. Wilmington, DE: ISI, 2003, p. 31.

18. Quoted in Neimark, *Myth Maker*, pp. 39–40.

19. Quoted in Neimark, *Myth Maker*, p. 37.

Chapter 3: Off to War

20. Quoted in Pearce, *Tolkien*, p. 144.

21. Quoted in Carpenter, *J.R.R. Tolkien*, p. 82.

22. Quoted in Pearce, *Tolkien*, p. 75.

23. Quoted in Carpenter, *J.R.R. Tolkien*, p. 94.

24. Quoted in Birzer, *J.R.R. Tolkien's Sanctifying Myth*, pp. 31–32.

25. Quoted in Pearce, *Tolkien*, p. 77.

26. Quoted in Pearce, *Tolkien*, p. 76.

Chapter 4: The Professor

27. Quoted in Birzer, *J.R.R. Tolkien's Sanctifying Myth*, p. 28.

28. Quoted in Birzer, *J.R.R. Tolkien's Sanctifying Myth*, p. 4.

29. Quoted in Michael White, *Critical Lives: J.R.R. Tolkien*. Indianapolis, IN: Alpha, 2002, p. 127.

30. Quoted in Shippey, *J.R.R. Tolkien*, p. xiii.

31. Quoted in Pearce, *Tolkien*, p. 184.

Chapter 5: The Inklings

32. Quoted in Shippey, *J.R.R. Tolkien*, p. 240.

33. Quoted in Carpenter, *J.R.R. Tolkien*, p. 114.

34. Quoted in Grotta, *J.R.R. Tolkien*, p. 91.

35. Quoted in Michael Coren, *J.R.R. Tolkien: The Man Who Created* The Lord of the Rings. New York: Scholastic, 2001, p. 62.

36. Quoted in Becker, *The Tolkien Scrapbook,* p. 36.

37. Quoted in Becker, *The Tolkien Scrapbook,* p. 32.

38. Quoted in Ang, *The Master of the Rings,* p. 45.

39. Quoted in Neimark, *Myth Maker,* p. 63.

40. Quoted in Becker, *The Tolkien Scrapbook,* p. 29.

41. Quoted in Pearce, *Tolkien,* p. 2.

42. Grotta, *J.R.R. Tolkien,* p. 78.

43. Quoted in Carpenter, *J.R.R. Tolkien,* p. 138.

44. Quoted in Coren, *J.R.R. Tolkien,* p. 74.

45. Quoted in Becker, *The Tolkien Scrapbook,* p. 34.

Chapter 6: The Lord of the Rings

46. Quoted in Carpenter, *J.R.R. Tolkien,* p. 188.

47. Quoted in Neimark, *Myth Maker,* p. 68.

48. Quoted in Grotta, *J.R.R. Tolkien,* p. 107.

49. Quoted in Birzer, *J.R.R. Tolkien's Sanctifying Myth,* p. 27.

50. Quoted in Becker, *The Tolkien Scrapbook,* p. 35.

51. Quoted in Neimark, *Myth Maker,* p. 79.

52. Quoted in Carpenter and Tolkien, *The Letters of J.R.R. Tolkien,* p. 163.

53. Quoted in Neimark, *Myth Maker,* p. 82.

54. Quoted in Carpenter, *J.R.R. Tolkien,* p. 221.

55. C.S. Lewis, "The Gods Return to Earth," *Time and Tide,* August 15, 1954, p. 24.

56. Edmund Wilson, "Oo, Those Awful Orcs!" *Nation,* April 14, 1956, p. 36.

57. Quoted in Neimark, *Myth Maker,* p. 84.

58. Quoted in Birzer, *J.R.R. Tolkein's Sanctifying Myth,* p. 15.

59. Quoted in Carpenter, *J.R.R. Tolkien,* p. 226.

60. Quoted in Grotta, *J.R.R. Tolkien,* p. 120.

Chapter 7: The Later Years

61. Quoted in Pearce, *Tolkien,* p. 6.

62. Quoted in Birzer, *J.R.R. Tolkien's Sanctifying Myth,* p. 12.

63. Quoted in White, *Critical Lives,* p. 244.

64. J.R.R. Tolkien, *The Fellowship of the Ring.* New York: Ballantine, 1965, p. 12.

65. Quoted in Carpenter, *J.R.R. Tolkien,* p. 232.

66. Quoted in White, *Critical Lives,* p. 234.

67. Quoted in Grotta, *J.R.R. Tolkien,* p. 142.

68. Quoted in Grotta, *J.R.R. Tolkien,* p. 156.

69. *"The Silmarillion* by J.R.R. Tolkien," *Washington Post,* September 11, 1977, p. E2.

Epilogue: The Legacy

70. Quoted in Becker, *The Tolkien Scrapbook,* p. 36.

71. Quoted in Pearce, *Tolkien,* p. 87.

72. Quoted in Pearce, *Tolkien,* p. 111.

73. Jess Cagle, "Lure of the Rings," *Time,* November 23, 2002, p. 32.

74. Quoted in Shippey, *J.R.R. Tolkien,* p. xviii.

75. Quoted in Grotta, *J.R.R. Tolkien,* p. 122.

76. Quoted in Pearce, *Tolkien,* p. 196.

For Further Reading

Susan Ang, *The Master of the Rings*. Cambridge, England: Icon, 2002. A very easy-to-read book broken up into sections on Tolkien's life and a discussion of his works.

Jess Cagle, "Lure of the Rings," *Time,* November 23, 2002. An article that takes a thorough look at the making of the New Line Cinema films based on the works of J.R.R. Tolkien.

David Colbert, *The Magical Worlds of* The Lord of the Rings. New York: Berkley, 2002. Designed to give readers a further insight to the creation of Tolkien's epic adventure, this book presents well-researched information in a very accessible question-and-answer format.

Michael Coren, *J.R.R. Tolkien: The Man Who Created* The Lord of the Rings. New York: Scholastic, 2001. A condensed and easy-to-read survey of the life and works of J.R.R. Tolkien.

Anne E. Neimark, *Myth Maker: J.R.R. Tolkien*. Orlando, FL: Harcourt Brace, 1996. A biography of Tolkien in the form of a narrative children's story.

Brian Sibley, The Lord of the Rings: *The Making of the Movie Trilogy*. Boston: Houghton Mifflin, 2002. Through wonderful pictures and interviews, this book offers an in-depth look at the creation of the New Line Cinema version of Tolkien's epic.

Books by J.R.R. Tolkien

J.R.R. Tolkien, *The Father Christmas Letters*. Boston: Houghton Mifflin, 1976. A collection of letters Tolkien wrote to his children from 1920 through 1938, in which he pretended to be Father Christmas and told them of his amazing adventures at the North Pole.

———, *The Hobbit*. Boston: Houghton Mifflin, 1997. The classic story of a small creature named Bilbo Baggins who sets out on a quest of adventure. With a band of dwarves and a wizard to accompany him, Bilbo encounters trolls, dragons, treasure, and a magic ring.

———, *The Lord of the Rings*. Boston: Houghton Mifflin, 1987. An epic tale of adventure that chronicles the journey of the hobbit Frodo, who must travel to the heart of a great evil and destroy a powerful and dangerous magic ring.

———, *The Monsters and the Critics and Other Essays*. Boston: Houghton Mifflin, 1984. A collection of essays by Tolkien, including his famous lecture on *Beowulf.*

———, *The Silmarillion*. Boston: Houghton Mifflin, 1998. The collected history and epic myths of the first and second ages of Middle Earth.

———, *The Tolkien Reader*. New York: Ballantine Books, 1966. A collection of short works by J.R.R. Tolkien, including his famous lecture "On Fairy-Stories."

Web Sites

Tolkien in Oxford. www.jrrtolkien.org.uk. This informative Web site provides detailed information on the life of J.R.R. Tolkien. While it focuses primarily on his life in Oxford, it covers a number of other aspects of his life as well.

The Barrow-Downs. www.barrowdowns.com. A comprehensive guide to the history and lore of Middle Earth. The site contains an encyclopedia of detailed information on any name, place, or object in Middle Earth. It also provides artwork, language studies, reader polls, and links to other sites.

The J.R.R. Tolkien Information Page. www.csclub.uwaterloo.ca. This Web site offers a large number of links to other Tolkien-related resources. It includes personal pages, translations, discussion forums, Tolkien groups, and biographical information.

The One Ring.net. www.theonering.net. The largest and most up-to-date Internet source on *The Lord of the Rings* films. It has press releases, discussion forums, and links to many other Tolkien-related sites.

Works Consulted

Books

Alida Becker, *The Tolkien Scrapbook*. Philadelphia: Running, 1978. A very thorough look at the life of Tolkien, as well as the many critical essays that have been written about his work.

Bradley J. Birzer, *J.R.R. Tolkien's Sanctifying Myth*. Wilmington, DE: ISI, 2003. A discussion of Tolkien's life and the influences of his religious and political beliefs on his work.

Humphrey Carpenter, *J.R.R. Tolkien: A Biography*. New York: Houghton Mifflin, 2000. The only officially authorized biographer of Tolkien, Carpenter was granted complete access to all of Tolkien's letters and manuscripts, as well as interviews with all family members and friends.

Humphrey Carpenter and Christopher Tolkien, eds., *The Letters of J.R.R. Tolkien*. New York: Houghton Mifflin, 2000. A comprehensive collection of letters written by Tolkien throughout his life, touching on everything from the writing of his works of fiction to his personal relationships. Edited by Tolkien's authorized biographer and Tolkien's son Christopher.

G.D.H. Cole and T.W. Earp, eds., *Oxford Poetry*. Oxford: B.H. Blackwell, 1915. An anthology including Tolkien's first published poem, "Goblin Feet."

Daniel Grotta, *J.R.R. Tolkien: Architect of Middle Earth*. Philadelphia: Running, 1992. An unauthorized biography of the life and times of J.R.R. Tolkien

Jared Lobdell, *A Tolkien Compass*. Peru, IL: Open Court, 1975. A collection of essays on Tolkien's work, exploring themes such as morality, corruption, and the history of Western literature.

Joseph Pearce, *Tolkien: A Celebration*. San Francisco: Ignatius, 2001. A collection of essays and interviews discussing a variety of Tolkien-related topics ranging from discussions of his life to critical analyses of his books.

Tom Shippey, *J.R.R. Tolkien: Author of the Century*. New York: Houghton Mifflin, 2000. Written by a fellow Oxford linguist, this book focuses on the themes and linguistic derivations of Tolkien's work and how his life helped to shape these influences.

—— *The Road to Middle Earth*. London: Grafton, 1992. A biographical sketch of Tolkien's life and creation of his epic works of fantasy.

Mark Eddy Smith, *Tolkien's Ordinary Virtues*. Downers Grove, IL: InterVarsity, 2002. This book takes a look at the simple spiritual themes that can be found throughout the works of J.R.R. Tolkien.

Michael White, *Critical Lives: J.R.R. Tolkien*. Indianapolis, IN: Alpha, 2002. A biography on the life and impact of Tolkien.

Periodicals

W.H. Auden, "At the End of the Quest, Victory," *New York Times Book Review*, January 22, 1956. Famous British poet Auden, an admirer of Tolkien, issued this early glowing review of *The Lord of the Rings* shortly after the final volume was released in 1955.

Joy Hill, "Echoes of the Old Ringmaster," *London Times*, December 10, 1990. Tolkien's former secretary discusses her relationship with the old professor.

C.S. Lewis, "The Gods Return to Earth," *Time and Tide*, August 15, 1954. A highly complimentary review of *The Fellowship of the Ring* by Tolkien's colleague and friend.

Jonathon Sales, "All Smials," *The Guardian*, September 10, 1977. A favorable review of *The Silmarillion*.

"The Silmarillion by J.R.R. Tolkien," *Washington Post*, September 11, 1977. One of the first reviews of *The Silmarillion*, upon its release four years after Tolkien's death.

Edmund Wilson, "Oo, Those Awful Orcs!" *Nation*, April 14, 1956. A scathing review of *The Lords of the Rings* by an influential critic and important voice among Tolkien detractors.

Index

as Merton Professor, 76
messages read into work
    of, 15, 16, 94–95
military service of, 13,
    41–44
in the orphanage, 25–26
perfectionism of, 48, 50,
    54, 59, 61, 76, 79
poetry of, 32, 36, 40–41,
    46, 47, 85
reactions of, to
    criticism, 63
rejection feared by, 61
retirement of, 15, 85
speech impediment of, 68
stories "revealed" to, 14,
    45, 46, 75
as a teacher/lecturer,
    54–56, 68
trees loved by, 19–20, 83
trench fever of, 44
tutoring job of, 52
undergraduate studies
    of, 13, 33–36, 39, 40
visit of, to childhood
    home, 23

Tolkien, Mabel Suffield
    (mother), 17–20, 21,
    22–25
Tolkien, Michael (son), 59,
    64, 76
Tolkien, Priscilla
    (daughter), 58, 83
Tolkien in Oxford
    (documentary), 89
Tolkien Societies, 86, 87
Tolkien Society of
    America, 88
Tom Bombadil (fictional
    character), 65
Tree and Leaf, 78
Two Towers, The (book),
    44, 80
Two Towers, The (film), 95

United States, Tolkien's
    work in, 71, 80, 85–86
Unwin, Rayner, 69, 70–71,
    76–78, 79–80
Unwin, Stanley, 70–71, 78, 79

Valar (angels), 95
Valinor (fictional location),
    47, 61
Viking Club, 54
*Voyage of Earendel the
    Evening Star, The* (poem),
    36, 40, 45–47

Warwick (England), 38, 39
Washington Post
    (newspaper), 93
Waterstone's Booksellers, 12
Welsh (language), 22, 28,
    35, 47, 54
West Midland County
    (England), 27, 48
Wheel of Time (Jordan), 15
White, Michael, 37
Wilson, Edmund, 80, 81
Wiseman, Christopher, 25,
    29, 30, 32, 47, 61
Wizard of Oz, The (Baum), 96
World War I, 13, 40, 41–44
World War II, 76, 94
Wright, Joseph, 29, 35, 36, 37

Picture Credits

Cover: Retna
AP/Wide World Photo, 81, 88
The Art Archive, 31, 70
Camera Press/Pamela Chandler/Retna, 15, 77, 84, 92
Camera Press/Retna, 23

© Christie's Images/CORBIS, 74
© ReutersNewMedia/CORBIS, 96
© Hulton Archive/Getty Images, 13, 14, 20, 21, 28, 34, 42, 51, 62, 66
Mary Evans Picture library, 55

About the Author

Stuart P. Levine has written a number of nonfiction books on topics ranging from endangered animals to Dr. Seuss. Holding degrees in wildlife education and psychology, he currently works as a conservation educator at a zoological institution in central Florida.